Making Sense of Theory and Practice in Early Childhood

Making Sense of Theory and Practice in Early Childhood

The Power of Ideas

Edited by

Tim Waller, Judy Whitmarsh and Karen Clarke

 Open University Press

Open University Press
McGraw-Hill Education
McGraw-Hill House
Shoppenhangers Road
Maidenhead
Berkshire
England
SL6 2QL

email: enquiries@openup.co.uk
world wide web: www.openup.co.uk

and Two Penn Plaza, New York, NY 10121-2289, USA

First published 2011

Copyright © Tim Waller, Judy Whitmarsh and Karen Clarke 2011

A catalogue record of this book is available from the British Library

ISBN-13: 978 0 335 24246 7 (pb) / 978 0 335 24247 4 (hb)
ISBN-10: 0 335 24246 4 (pb) / 0 335 24247 2 (hb)

eISBN-13: 978 0 335 24248 1
eISBN-10: 0 335 24248 0

Library of Congress Cataloging-in-Publication Data
CIP data has been applied for

Fictitous names of companies, products, people, characters and/or data that may be used herein (in case studies or in examples) are not intended to represent any real individual, company, product or event.

Typeset by Aptara Inc., India
Printed in Great Britain by CPI Antony Rowe, Chippenham, Wiltshire

The McGraw·Hill Companies

Contents

PART 2
Structure, power and knowledge

List of figures and table

Figures

Table

Author biographies

Angeliki Bitou is an early years teacher in Greece and a PhD student at the University of Wolverhampton, studying curriculum and pedagogy for children under 3 years old. She completed her MSc in Early Childhood Studies at the University of Wales, Swansea. Her research interests are in how children under 3 years old experience the planning of activities in day-care, making a comparison between settings in England and Greece.

Liz Brooker was an early years teacher in Inner London for many years before returning to research and teaching in higher education (HE) at the Institute of Education in London, where she has responsibilities for masters and doctoral courses. Her research has focused on the experiences of children and families as they make transitions into and between education and care settings in the years from birth to 5. She is also currently involved in coediting a series, Early Childhood in Focus, which provides concise information on early education and care for policymakers and providers in international contexts.

Karen Clarke is Associate Dean for Teaching and Learning in the School of Education, University of Wolverhampton. She is responsible for curriculum development in early years, special needs and inclusion studies and education studies. Karen's recent research has focused on language and communication development in young children, the relationship between oracy and writing skills in primary children, and issues around teaching and learning in HE: embedding study skills in first year undergraduate modules, developing students' reading and writing skills, and effective teaching and learning in HE. All these topics are influenced by a range of educational and sociocultural factors.

Sue Fawson is currently a senior lecturer in early primary teacher education at the University of Wolverhampton having previously lectured on the early childhood studies degree programmes and on childcare and education courses in further education. Sue's interest in early years originates from a career as an early years teacher in primary schools. Sue has been instrumental in developing the foundation degree in early childhood studies and the BEd degree in early primary teacher education. Her research interests include art and child development – the role of art in the development of the whole child; the impact of artists in residence; assessment of art and design in the primary school; young children's learning within art gallery spaces; children as drawers.

Rohan Jowallah's research interests have focused particularly around issues relating to literacy, language and inclusion. His interests are based on his social constructionist perspective of development. Rohan has international experience of having taught in Jamaica, England and the USA within the public education systems. Based on this, he also has interest in comparative issues relating to literacy and inclusion. Rohan recently completed his doctorate focusing on the utilization of critical literacy within the National Curriculum in England. In addition, Rohan has published several articles in peer-reviewed journals and has presented at international conferences.

Maggie Leese is a principal lecturer and head of department for childhood and family studies at the University of Wolverhampton. Her background was in children's nursing for many years before completing a degree in early childhood and more recently an MA in social work specializing in children and families. Maggie is currently studying at PhD level and her research focuses on family support within inter-professional teams and the social construction of parenting.

Martin Needham trained and worked as an early years teacher in Nottinghamshire, London and Pakistan. This was followed by four years as an early years development officer for a local authority working on a range of initiatives including early years development and childcare partnerships, children's information services, foundation stage, neighbourhood nurseries, quality assurance and children's centres. He became a senior lecturer in early childhood studies in 2003. Martin is currently undertaking research into forums that encourage parents and practitioners to exchange views about interactions with children aged 1 and 2. Martin has published work on multiagency working (in Siraj-Blatchford, Clarke and Needham, *The Team around the Child* (Trentham Books 2007).

Jane O'Connor is a senior lecturer in early childhood studies at the University of Wolverhampton. Her background is in education and she is an experienced primary school teacher as well as an academic. She completed her doctorate at Brunel University and is the author of *The Cultural Significance of the Child Star* (Routledge 2008). Her research interests lie with representations of children in the media, especially 'exceptional' children, and in the area of gifted and talented education.

Lynn Richards is a senior lecturer in early childhood studies at the University of Wolverhampton. Her background is in working with children, young people, and their families in a variety of provisions: early years settings, playschemes, youth clubs, and community projects. Lynn's research interests include issues to do with equitable practices, particularly in the area of race and social justice; she is keen to explore the attitudinal dispositions that the workforce brings to bear on the educative process.

Faye Stanley worked in several early years settings in Birmingham for education and social services departments and taught in a primary school for six years. She is now a senior lecturer in childhood and family studies at Wolverhampton University where she is module leader for 'Continuing the Learning: The Curriculum for Children 5–8 Years' and 'Enjoy and Achieve through Play'. Her research interests involve quality in early years education, cross-national studies and the curriculum for children aged birth to 11 years and children's experiences of pedagogical interaction.

Tim Waller is reader in early years education at the University of Wolverhampton. He was formerly Director of Postgraduate Studies in the Department of Childhood Studies at Swansea University. Previously he taught in nursery, infant and primary schools in London and has also worked in the USA. His research interests include ICT and social justice, outdoor learning and pedagogy. He completed his doctoral thesis on scaffolding young children's learning and ICT. Since September 2003 he has been coordinating a research project designed to investigate the promotion of children's wellbeing through outdoor play. He is also co-directing the Longitudinal Evaluation of the Role and Impact of Early Years Professional Status (EYPS) for the Children's Workforce Development Council (CWDC). Tim edited the second edition of *An Introduction to Early Childhood: A multidisciplinary approach* (Sage 2009).

Judy Whitmarsh is a post-doctoral research fellow at the Centre for the Development of Applied Research in Education (University of Wolverhampton). With a background in both health and teaching, her research interests focus on the interface between education, health and social care. Her doctoral thesis explored maternal knowledge and understanding of infant speech and language development, underpinned by a sociological argument about perceptions of 'good' mothering. She has published articles based on themes that emerged in her thesis as well as her current research interests. Judy has been involved in research projects on obesity in primary schools, a city-wide strategy to transform school food, leisure facilities for children and young people with disabilities, and parental perceptions of partnerships in the early years. She has contributed a chapter to the book on multiagency working by Siraj-Blatchford, Clarke and Needham, *The Team around the Child* (Trentham Books 2007).

Jo Winwood is a senior lecturer and subject leader in special needs and inclusion studies at the University of Wolverhampton. Her background is in education in a range of mainstream and specialist provisions. Her current research interests revolve around the development of inclusive practices, with a particular focus on the role of the special educational needs coordinator (SENCO).

Gill Woods started her teaching career in Birmingham and worked in three primary schools, predominantly teaching Foundation and Key Stage 1 children. Since transferring to higher education she has taught PGCE and undergraduate students mathematics and ICT, and professional studies to students training to teach in the early years. Her research interests include the understanding and use of mathematical language of Foundation Stage children, the development of social skills, peer tutoring and the impact of the Every Child Matters agenda upon schools.

Jenny Worsley is a senior lecturer in early childhood studies at Wolverhampton University. Her background is embedded in early years education, primarily as a practitioner in a variety of early years settings, including community day provision, schools, nursery and playgroups. Her research interests include pedagogical issues surrounding children's play, and the development of professionalism and quality of practice in early years services. Her most recent research has involved blended learning pedagogy and the use of online resources to support transition of part-time mature students into higher education.

Foreword
Professor Christine Pascal and Professor Tony Bertram

This book appears at a significant time for those who work in early childhood services as they undergo a radical process of expansion, transformation and improvement. In early childhood there is a sharper need than ever to bring to-gether theory and practice to ensure this change process is the result of careful thought and informed professional knowledge. In our work in the field we re-spect Bourdieu's claim that 'I never theorize if that is to engage in "conceptual gobbledygook" or use a set of theories in their own right' (Bourdieu 1990: 32). We like his notion of theories being a set of 'thinking tools' which are to be gained and used as part of a practical engagement with empirical, real world situations and problems. For us there is no separation of practice and theory and we agree with Kurt Lewin (1949, quoted in Hunt 1987: 4) that 'there is nothing so practical as a good theory'. Our aim is to theorize practice and in this sense all our work aims to be an 'act of practical theory'.

In this sharp and reflective book, we can see a set of authors who mirror this position on the synergy between theory and practice in early childhood beautifully. They demonstrate that it is strengthening to be able to lean heavily on the powerful ideas of others who have been interested in similar kinds of theoretical and professional struggles. It is a wonderful tribute that through this book we in the sector can acknowledge the huge debt we all have to the gurus who provide us with an engine house of ideas to think and act with. It is interesting that the contributions in this book draw on the ideas of those who have heavily influenced our work too. In particular, those who feature in our own reflections include Anthony Giddens from England, Paulo Freire from Brazil, Pierre Bourdieu from France, and Jerome Bruner from the USA – an international set of core influences from the multidisciplinary fields of sociological, political and psychological research.

The authors in this book have succeeded in putting reflexivity and praxis at the heart of their work. By reflexivity we mean more than just benign introspection or reflection on what we are doing or plan to do. We use the term in a Bourdieuan sense of trying to achieve a 'situated understanding' of the field and our place and role within it. This demands critical scrutiny of every action we take as researchers and writers. The reflexivity also allows us to operate in praxis, by which we mean living out an intimate and ongoing relationship between reflection and action. We reflect in order to act and when we act we have to think. This process is iterative and ongoing at all stages in our work. The narratives in this book are excellent examples of this process in action.

This book is important because it demonstrates the power of ideas and the potential energy which is released when theory and practice come together, increasing the impact and complexity of the narratives of practice that result. Each chapter provides a detailed exemplar of how theory and practice intertwine within the narrative as the author seeks to explain and understand the complexities of the real world in its many guises. As such it is both timely and enormously helpful to those in the field who are attempting to cross the theory/practice divide. The group of authors who have collaborated to produce this edited book are respected researchers, writers and activists in the field of early childhood. The authors have come together to create this collection and in doing so they demonstrate the benefits of sharing expertise in thinking and developing reflective services. The blend of scholarship and the rigour of the research in this collection of chapters is a model for others to follow. They have succeeded in making this expert knowledge accessible and directly relevant to those concerned with developing the quality of policy and practice in the field. We believe their joint work will make an important contribution to transforming current policy and practice and in enabling practitioners and policymakers to talk more powerful in the language of 'possibilities'.

References

Bourdieu, P. (1990) *The Logic of Practice*, trans. R. Nice. Cambridge: Polity.
Hunt, D.E. (1987) *Beginning with Ourselves: In practice, theory and human affairs.* Cambridge, MA: Brookline.

Introduction

Tim Waller, Judy Whitmarsh and Karen Clarke

The idea for this book emerged from discussions within the Childhood Research Cluster at the University of Wolverhampton: a fluid group of university postgraduate students, lecturers, academics and researchers who all have a focus on teaching and research with children in their early years and their families. The cluster members have a variety of professional backgrounds including early years practice, teaching, social work, psychology and school health. This wide knowledge base brings with it a range of experiences of research and practice, however the cluster also has a focus on creating an effective learning environment and a culture of critical exploration for students in the School of Education, whether foundation, undergraduate, masters or doctoral students. Not only are the chapter authors senior lecturers and postgraduate supervisors, but also they are all involved in a personal research journey which has underpinned their contribution to the book.

The central theme of the book, the integration of powerful ideas within theory and their application to practice, arose from the learning trajectories of the contributors and also from their experiences of working with students. We wanted to challenge students to look beyond the traditional theories of early childhood, to be excited by discovering that there is more to Vygotsky, for example, than just the zone of proximal development, to consider theoretical concepts not necessarily associated with early childhood, and above all, we hope to show that theory can be exciting, innovative and applied in different ways to different aspects of the research process to trigger new ways of thinking.

During our personal research journeys, we found that many of us had experienced a distinct trajectory of development in relation to theory: beginning with the 'fear and dread' and 'I cannot do theory' stage, we then moved on to reading huge numbers of 'how to' books, which left us even more overwhelmed. An academic supervisor or more knowledgeable colleague might then suggest that we try reading an eminent theorist or two, while we desperately search for the 'correct' theory to fit our research project. It is only when, quite suddenly, we experience a Eureka moment, realizing that a theoretical 'powerful idea' makes sense to us, is coherent with our experiences, and/or will inform our research that theory becomes an integral part of who we are as researchers.

It is our understanding that there is no 'one-size-fits-all' theory in relation to early years research, but rather that we choose to create a research pathway which draws on concepts from a range of theories and theoretical concepts; as Pirrie and Macleod (2010: 370) highlight 'tripping, slipping and losing the way' tells us something about the researcher and the environment in which the research is conducted. The contributors to this book demonstrate how theory can underpin research and practice in a variety of ways: to demonstrate links with practice, to support data analysis and as a conceptual framework. They also describe some of the slips, trips and false turns which they have made in their research journey before showing how some of these apparent detours led to serendipitous moments of discovery.

Overview of the book

The book is divided into two parts: in Part 1, there are six chapters which explore a group of related 'social constructivist' ideas that stem from psychological investigations of how an individual's learning is informed by interaction with a social community. The ideas presented in these chapters can be used to help structure investigations of the way learners are influenced by, not only by those around them, but also by the social environment. Since the late 1970s, 'social constructivist' ideas have become increasingly influential and visible in theories of learning and teaching (Alexander 2008) and, for example, are now central to the Early Years Foundation Stage (Department for Children, Schools and Families (DCSF) 2008) in England.

Each chapter contributes less familiar but increasingly influential ideas emanating from Vygotskian theory. These ideas are used to explore how individuals interact with others and how both parties might be influenced by this interactive exchange or 'dialectic process'.

Part 1: Community, interaction and identity

In Part 1, each chapter takes an element from a well-known sociocultural investigator and shows how this might be used in a research context. The author first describes the background to the powerful theoretical idea or theorist before showing how this has been used within the research or practice. At the end of each chapter, there is a guided reading section.

In Chapter 1, Faye Stanley introduces Vygotsky's key ideas but concentrates in particular on his lesser known work on children's use of vocalized self-directing speech (Vygotsky 1986). Faye draws on the work of Vygotsky and discusses its relationship with the work of Piaget; she highlights the importance of the self-directed speech of young children and supports the argument that the modelling of language to children is vitally important.

Next, in Chapter 2, Lynn Richards explores the power of story and the characters it creates through the work of Jerome Bruner (2007). Drawing on Bruner, Lynn discusses the power of words to contribute to social realities and the potential of culture to control meaning. Using examples from her own research into constructions of 'whiteness' in the narratives of early years practitioners, she seeks to uncover embedded cultural scripts and norms.

Sue Fawson and Gill Woods, in Chapter 3, bring us Howard Gardner's powerful ideas about the existence and framework of multiple intelligences. Sue and Gill show us how Gardner's ideas emerged to counter Piaget's notions of intelligence (and IQ testing) yet have developed throughout his long career, somewhat like those of his peer, Jerome Bruner, in Chapter 2. The authors offer us an excellent overview of Gardner the man, as well as a critique of his concepts and some common misunderstandings in the interpretation of his work. They conclude with case studies to illustrate how Gardner's theoretical concepts can be applied to support practice.

In Chapter 4, Martin Needham discusses Vygosky's concept of 'activity' and how human action has evolved through the development of tools and ideas. Drawing on his doctoral research, Martin explores how contemporary investigators such as Rogoff (1990) and Engeström (2007) demonstrate how theoretical concepts can complement the analysis of research methods, such as observation, and allow us to 'dig deeper' to show how parents, children and practitioners may have different understandings of the purpose of a preschool activity. It is suggested that by studying these differences we may help people to support each other more effectively.

Jenny Worsley explores the importance of a community of practice in Chapter 5. She studies the work of Jean Lave and Etienne Wenger (Lave and Wenger 1991) who develop the idea that individuals need to learn more than the basics to perform an activity, they also need to learn the social etiquette, rules and local languages to perform effectively as part of a team. During Jenny's doctoral research into supporting foundation degree students, she and colleagues have developed a series of planned student blogs; in the chapter, she explores how these have contributed to the development of a community of practice and the potential benefits of this, particularly for non-traditional higher education students.

In the final chapter of Part 1 (Chapter 6), Liz Brooker examines the emergence of the concept of learning dispositions; she further discusses how post-Vygotskian thinkers, such as Gordon Wells and Guy Claxton (Wells and

Claxton 2002), draw attention to the importance of children being encouraged to develop positive learning dispositions. Using a case-study approach, Liz offers some suggestions about how theoretical concepts of learning dispositions can be applied both to research and practice and can support observation and deeper knowledge of the child.

Part 2: Structure, power and knowledge

The second part of this book moves into a more poststructuralist, critical, consideration of power, knowledge and structure in the world of the child. Poststructuralists, such as Michel Foucault and Pierre Bourdieu, while not focusing their work directly on children, have much to offer childhood studies by challenging our existing ways of thinking and how we perceive the 'truths' and the 'facts' of child development.

Globalization and the increasing movement of families around the world, together with social inequities and inequality within the UK, offer us the opportunity to radically rethink traditionally held beliefs about how we perceive childhood, diversity, inclusion, and discourses of normalization (MacNaughton 2005; Robinson and Jones Diaz 2006). As Dahlberg et al. (2007: xiv) observe, reading some theorists can be difficult because their writing may be dense and highly academic; their thoughts can also be 'highly provocative, disorientating and unsettling'. However, as theorists such as Levinas and Baumann (see Dahlberg et al. 2007: 36–39) argue, it is by troubling our relationships with the Other and by listening that we contest universalism.

Chapter 7 begins with Tim Waller and Angeliki Bitou's discussion of how our understanding of childhood has emerged and altered; moving beyond the psychological, essentialist, view of the child (and childhood) as a fixed developmental stage in the process of becoming an adult, Tim and Angeliki illustrate how children are capable of both forming and being formed by circumstances and social phenomena (James et al. 1998).

Reflecting critically on the sociocultural perspective, that children and adults are co-constructors of their joint experiences, Tim and Angeliki draw on the work of Barbara Rogoff (for example, Rogoff 2003) and William Corsaro to explore the concepts of agency and participation in relation to the early years of childhood. Making reference to case studies from a preschool setting in Greece and from an outdoor learning project in the UK, Angeliki and Tim analyse children's play using a theoretical lens from the studies of Rogoff and Corsaro. They engage in a critique of the concepts of agency and participation to demonstrate how insights from the new sociology of childhood can complement sociocultural perspectives to aid our understanding of the play and learning of young children.

Jane O'Connor, in Chapter 8, brings us a scholarly critique of the concepts of the French social theorist, Pierre Bourdieu, which have informed her own research. Using a case-study approach, Jane discusses the notions of cultural capital and habitus, demonstrating how, although contested, these can inform our understanding of early years practice.

Jane reviews a number of seminal studies which have used Bourdieu's concepts as a theoretical framework for research or as analytical tools. For example, she draws on Liz Brooker's earlier work (Brooker 2002) in inner-city schools to show how concepts from Bourdieu can illuminate and support our understanding of the different ways in which children 'do' school and how culture can support or inhibit the way in which teachers and practitioners perceive children's learning. Finally, Jane notes how a consideration of cultural capital and habitus can have implications for early years practice.

In Chapter 9, Rohan Jowallah revisits the work of Brazilian educationalist, Paulo Freire. Rohan's doctoral research is underpinned by critical literacy theory and he shows us how this has informed his study of the pedagogy of literacy. Taking Freire's conceptualization of literacy as more than just learning to read, Rohan demonstrates how language, thought and reality help to form an understanding of the social world for children (Freire 2005). Freire was a strong and fearless advocate of social justice and this underpinned the development of critical literacy theory. Rohan guides us through Freire's powerful ideas then considers how these cohere with notions of structure, power, emancipation and social equality. Finally, Rohan draws on case studies to develop some strategies for educators considering taking a critical literacy approach in the classroom. He demonstrates how this can underpin good inclusive practice and benefit children and teachers.

In Chapter 10, Maggie Leese draws on her doctoral research in children's centres in England to explore how the landscape of children's services has changed since 1999 and the implications this has for inter-professional working.

Maggie's research explores how children's centre staff, from a range of professional backgrounds, negotiate their roles together and with parents who receive children's centre services. Maggie takes concepts from the work of Michel Foucault, the French social theorist, to challenge the 'regimes of truth' traditionally accepted within early years practice; she shows how Foucault's thinking about how power, knowledge and truth operate within normalizing discourses can lead us to challenge these discourses and to reflect critically on relationships and practices in the early years. Using excerpts from her interviews with children's centre staff, Maggie deconstructs underlying dominant discourses of power and inequality within professional relationships. She also takes Foucauldian concepts to highlight how the discourse of the 'good' mother emerged and has come to politicized dominance.

Finally, in Chapter 11, Jo Winwood explores how an ethic of care is rel-evant to the early years. In her research, Jo has been exploring the role of the special educational needs coordinator (SENCO) and she has found the ethic of care a highly appropriate theoretical approach in its applicability to issues of inclusion. Jo traces the development of our conceptualization of moral decision-making from Gilligan's perspective (Gilligan 1993). Showing how the feminist perspective has challenged Kohlberg's gendered study, which appeared to find that men were morally superior to women, Jo demonstrates how the ethic of care blends interdependence and connectivity with mutually supportive relationships; however she argues that the target-driven ethos of our current educational system runs counter to the development of an ethic of care in schools. She further points out the difficulty for teachers in focusing on 'care' in an education setting.

As noted earlier, the editors and contributors to this book come from a variety of different professional backgrounds, just as the readers will not be a heterogeneous group; thus the perspectives cover a wide range of approaches, theories, and sites of practice. The interlinking theme is, however, the way in which their research is underpinned by theory and concepts from theorists. We cannot claim that the book is anything but a western perspective on theory but we hope that by the inclusion of research from more than one country and of theorists from across the world, we have shown that theory is global. We hope that we have demonstrated that theory is not a subject to fear but one which, if appropriately applied, can add depth and substance to research and challenge students to find different ways of thinking about research topics, methodology, analysis and participants.

References

Alexander, R. (2008) *Essays on Pedagogy.* London: Routledge.

Brooker, L. (2002) *Starting School: Young children learning cultures.* Buckingham: Open University Press.

Bruner, J. (2007) *Cultivating the Possible.* Oxford: Oxford University Press.

Dahlberg, G., Moss, P. and Pence, A. (2007) *Beyond Quality in Early Childhood Education and Care: Languages of evaluation,* 2nd edn. Abingdon: Routledge.

Department for Children, Schools and Families (DCSF) (2008) *The Early Years Foundation Stage: Setting the standards for learning, development and care for children from birth to five.* Nottingham: DCSF.

Engeström, Y. (2007) 'Putting Vygotsky to work.' In H. Daniels, M. Cole and J.V. Wertsch (eds) *The Cambridge Companion to Vygotsky.* New York: Cambridge University Press.

Freire, P. (2005) *Teachers as Cultural Workers: Letters to those who dare to teach.* Trans D. Macedo, D. Koike and A. Oliveira. Boulder, CO: Westview.

Gilligan, C. (1993) *In a Different Voice*. Cambridge, MA: Harvard University Press.

James, A., Jenks, C. and Prout, A. (1998) *Theorizing Childhood*. Cambridge: Polity.

Lave, J. and Wenger, E. (1991) *Situated Learning and Legitimate Peripheral Participation*. Cambridge: Cambridge University Press.

MacNaughton, G. (2005) *Doing Foucault in Early Childhood Studies: Applying post-structural ideas*. London: Routledge.

Pirrie, A. and Macleod, G. (2010) 'Tripping, slipping and losing the way: Moving beyond methodological difficulties in social research.' *British Educational Research Journal*, 36(3): 367–378.

Robinson, K.H. and Jones Diaz, C. (2006) *Diversity and Difference: Issues for theory and practice*. Maidenhead: Open University Press.

Rogoff, B. (1990) *Apprenticeship in thinking: Cognitive development in the social context*. New York: Open University Press.

Rogoff, B. (2003) *The Cultural Nature of Human Development*. Oxford: Oxford University Press.

Vygotsky, L.S. (1978) *Mind in Society*. Cambridge, MA: Harvard University Press.

Vygotsky, L.S. (1986) *Thought and Language*. Cambridge, MA: MIT Press.

Wells, G. and Claxton, G. (2002) *Learning for Life in the 21st Century*. London: Blackwell.

PART 1
Community, interaction and identity

1 Vygotsky – From public to private: learning from personal speech

Faye Stanley

Lev Semenovich Vygotsky (1896–1934) was born in Orso in the Russian Empire (present-day Belarus) into a non-religious Jewish family. Unfortunately, his life was short lived: he was 37 when he died in Moscow of tuberculosis. However, during his short life he was a pioneering psychologist and a highly prolific author. He graduated from Moscow State University in 1917 and he worked at the Institute of Psychology (from the mid-1920s) and other educational, research and clinical institutions in Moscow, Leningrad, and Kharkov where he worked extensively on ideas about cognitive development. Shortly after Vygotsky's death in 1934, the Stalin regime blacklisted his works for many years, but his ideas were preserved by his collaborators, especially A.R. Luria and A.N. Leontiev, and formed the foundation of Soviet 'socio-historical psychology'. His contributions are widely considered to be crucial to our understanding of the social nature of learning and have contributed significantly to western educational practices since the publication of his work in English in 1962.

Introduction

Although Vygotsky died in 1934, his work continues to make a significant impact upon the understanding of psychology throughout the world. In the Soviet Union (now Russia) Luria, Leontiev, Zinchenko and El'konin developed their own theories based on the foundations Vygotsky created (see Chapter 4). Modern psychology has preserved the heritage of Vygotsky's thinking, serving to deepen the principle ideas of the founder of this scientific school of thought in accordance with contemporary ideologies (Daniels 2001).

Vygotsky's written work covers a wide variety of areas but he was concerned most specifically with the development of the human mind. His critical and lasting insight was that there is an inseparable and organic connection, between individuals and their social circumstances, that is the source of thinking.

Vygotsky argued that 'it is as a result of social interactions between the growing child and other members of the child's community that the child acquires the tools of thinking and learning' (Smith et al. 1998: 426). In recent years, there has been an upsurge of interest in the ideas of Vygotsky and in western society in particular. This has mainly been due to his unique approach towards children's learning (Davydov and Zinchenko 1989). While Vygotsky's main theories relating to concepts of learning and development were not limited to any specific age, his best known ideas are often discussed in the context of young children (Kozulin et al. 2003) and have particular resonance for early years practitioners (Siraj-Blatchford 2007).

In particular, many scholars (for example, Stone 1998; Wells 1999; Daniels 2001) have sought to unravel Vygotsky's thinking of the zone of proximal development (ZPD). This is a process where a child's understanding is assisted by a 'more knowledgeable' person (discussed in more detail later on in this chapter). However, Vygotsky's theory of how children internalize their thoughts and their speech, progressing from public to private speech is far less researched. Berk (1992) claims that only seventeen studies have been carried out in relation to private speech and only seven of these have been published. Indeed, Vygotsky (1978: 25) highlights how 'the most significant moment in the course of intellectual development, which gives birth to the purely human forms of practical and abstract intelligence, occurs when speech and practical activity, two previously completely independent lines of development converge' (Vygotsky 1978: 25). This is illustrated in Figure 1.1.

The main discussion in this chapter concerns children aged 2–7 years focusing on the evolution of public to private speech and looking beyond this from a sociocultural perspective to provide some possible connections to practical application. This chapter illustrates the importance of shared communication between adults and children and observing children when they are beginning to internalize their thoughts and carrying out private speech utterances. The chapter is intended to provide insight into how students and

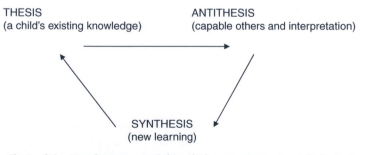

Figure 1.1 How language and thought become internalized. (Adapted from Vygotsky 1978: 54)

early years practitioners can make meaning of children's speech as they guide themselves through activities.

The origins of private speech

Vygotsky regarded private speech as 'a critical intermediate stage in the transition from external social communication to internal self direction and as the cornerstone of all higher cognitive processes, including selective attention, voluntary, memory, planning, concept formation and self reflection' (Berk 1992, quoted in Fernyhough and Lloyd 1999: 34). Thus for Vygotsky, the appearance of private speech at approximately 3 years of age originates in early socialized speech, which gradually separates into two functionally specific types: speech used to communicate with others and speech purely directed at the self. As private speech branches off from social speech, it becomes thought spoken out loud and 'an externalized self monitoring system, that plans, directs and controls behaviour' (Bivens and Berk 1990: 444). Once children are able to successfully bring action under the control of self-directed verbalizations, overt speech goes 'underground' turning into inner speech or verbal thought, which occurs at approximately 7 years of age (Berk and Landau 1993).

However, while Vygotsky conceptualized private speech as 'speech not to be addressed or adapted to a listener and which does not compel a reaction from a listener' (Berk and Garvin 1984: 271), Piaget's conception of this type of speech was quite different from that of Vygotsky. Piaget (1953) used the term 'egocentric speech' and he argued that egocentric speech represents a child's immaturity in taking into account the perspective of others. This reflects Piaget's (1953) theory of cognitive development. Piaget's view is constructivist, because he firmly believed that knowledge acquisition is a process of continuous self-construction. That is, knowledge is not out there, external to the child and waiting to be discovered. Instead, knowledge is invented and reinvented as the child develops and interacts with the surrounding world. While Piaget did not rule out the importance of the child's family (the social constructivist view) he placed less emphasis on this than Vygotsky (Smith et al. 1998). Essentially constructivist theory argues that knowledge is a 'web of relationships' and is constructed actively by learners as they attempt to make sense of their experiences and environments (Driscoll 2000).

During Piaget's (1953) observations regarding egocentric speech, he attempted to categorize all speech forms of children aged 6 years. He described eight categories in all and three of which he identified as being egocentric. The first categorization was repetition (echolalia) where a child's imitation of others words often completely unconscious. Second, he defined 'monologue', which is speech that accompanies action and a child often describes the action, the object of the action or a desire for something. Finally, he identified collective monologue which is essentially the same in context as monologue itself, but is marked with some indication that the child's intends to interest or thinks he/she is interesting to others in their thoughts or through the activities that they undertake (Zivin 1979). Thus according to Piaget, children rarely take their listener's perspective into account and he argued that egocentrism is the predominant factor of children's intellectual processes up until the age of 8 years (Zivin 1979). Indeed for Piaget it is not necessary for a listener to be present as before a child is able to think logically (what Piaget (1953) termed the 'pre-operational' stage) children display no social speech in social situations because they are unable to shift perspectives (decentre) from themselves to others. The child in Piaget's view is unwilling to become involved in the communicative process (Zivin 1979).

Piaget (1953) therefore believed that private speech expresses itself in a totally different form and that egocentric (private speech) represents a lack of communicative intent. Thus rejecting the view of the merging of language and thought postulated by Vygotsky. Conversely, Vygotsky (1978) argues that as preschool children gradually become able to appreciate the view of others, such speech decreases, as it becomes replaced by 'truly socialised communication' and this is a 'developmental achievement indicative of the school aged child's new capacity for reflective thought' (Bivens and Berk 1990: 443).

The following example illustrates how a 3-year-old boy engages in private speech to guide himself through a task:

> Jack is in the garden, in the dirt playing with several Bob the Builder diggers. Previous to this he had read a book on diggers and discussed what each vehicle does to build a road. He lines the diggers up in the soil. He then starts to sing (to the theme of 'Here we go round the Mulberry Bush'. 'I am going to dig up the land, dig up the land, dig up the land, I am going to dig up the land on a Wednesday morning. I am going to put safety cones around, safety cones around I am going to put safety cones around to keep all the people safe. I am then going to flatten it, flatten it, flatten it. I am then going to flatten it to make the land nice and flat. I am going to build a flat road build a flat road build a flat road, I am going to build a flat road on a sunny Wednesday morning. My work is now done for the day, done for the day, done for the day, my work is now done for the day and the road is ready to drive on.'

For Vygotsky (1978), at first private speech follows an action, occurring as an afterthought (as illustrated by Jack in the example above). Then speech occurs simultaneously with behaviour and during these two phases it is largely an accompaniment to the child's activity. Finally private speech moves towards the starting point of action and assumes a self-regulatory function through a child planning and modulating their behaviour on a moment-by-moment basis, as they grapple with challenging tasks. As mastery over behaviour improves, structural changes in private speech occur. Once private speech differentiates from social speech it need no longer occur in a fully expanded linguistic form, since adults as well as more able peers help children accomplish culturally meaningful activities, socially generated tools of thought, semantic knowledge, problem-solving procedures and meta cognitive strategies are incorporated into children's private speech and consequently into their thinking (Vygotsky 1978). According to Kozulin et al. (2003: 160), 'from using complete sentences typical for social speech, a child's utterances change into abbreviated phrases and single words unsuited for the purposes of communication to other people. But sufficient for communication with oneself' (again as illustrated by Jack in the example above).

Vyogtsky (1987) discussed how this major change in a child's private speech occurs during their preschool years. Thus in Vygotsky's theory, 'private speech is both the precursor of conscious self regulatory thought and a critical link in the cultural transmission of cognitive skills from one generation to the next' (Berk 1992, quoted in Fernyhough and Lloyd 1999: 34).

It can be seen that Piaget and Vygotsky's theories differ in a number of ways. Piaget's idea is that egocentric speech utterances represent a lack of communicative intent; Vygotsky on the other hand postulated that speech for oneself reflects a 'parasocial' will to communicate. Vygotsky believes that the child is able to distinguish between themself as the speaker and an external listener. The child is parasocial in that they do not distinguish themselves both as a listener and as an external listener. Therefore, according to Vygotsky, early self-guiding speech is in fact overt (Zivin 1979). Thus because Vygotsky had such a different view of egocentric speech from that of Piaget, it was relabelled private speech. As a way of synthesizing these two different perspectives, this chapter calls this speech 'personalised speech' which, as Kozulin et al. (2003: 156) define, is speech which goes 'from public to private speech'. I feel this offers a clearer view of what this chapter is aiming to exemplify.

Kohlberg et al. (1968) have also attempted to resolve the differences between Piaget and Vygotsky's unitary conceptualizations, particularly in relation to Piaget's view that private speech enhances self-guidance. Kohlberg et al. (1968) focused heavily on the work of Mead (1934), who supports Vygotsky's ideas, that private speech is assumed to have a cognitive self-guiding and self-communicative function. Mead 1934 (quoted in Berk and Garvin 1984: 167) states that speech and thought always have dialogue forms and functions and that knowledge by children of the meaning of their own actions occurs in the development of attempting to communicate that meaning to others. According to Mead (1934), young children can see themselves only from the perspective of others. This process actually begins by children describing their own actions to others and by calling out in themselves their implied response.

Subsequently, during this process, children begin to distinguish between the speaking self, from the self being talked to (Berk and Garvin 1984).

Kohlberg et al. (1968) developed six categories of private speech and provided evidence that they are part of a five-level developmental hierarchy. In this hierarchy, Piaget's (1929: 26) 'collective monologue' and 'monologue' are relabelled as 'describing one's own activity', because they are interpreted to be explanations of the self actions to a non-specific auditor, which is neither the self or the other. In other words, Kohlberg et al. (1968) suggest that private speech follows a curvilinear course of development and that it peaks earlier for more able children, thus concurring with the views of Vygotsky. For both Vygotsky (1978) and Kohlberg et al. (1968), children are constantly guided through verbal commands by others and as children attempt to control their own actions they imitate the same vocal method others have been using to help them. This again also emphasizes the important role the adult has to play in facilitating and expanding children's personalized speech, which is discussed later on in this chapter.

Moreover, to clarify the difference between social and private (personalized) speech, private speech in contrast to social speech is defined as 'speech addressed to the self (not to others) for the purpose of self regulation (rather than communication)' (Diaz and Berk 1992: 62). Additionally, Vygotsky (1978) claimed that at an early age, private speech and social speech were not clearly differentiated. Thus as the child gets older, the difference between social and private speech can be seen, by the gradual increase in syntactical form and loudness of private speech utterances. Vygotsky (1978) implied that during the course of development, private speech becomes more and more distinguishable from social speech. However, Wertsch (1979, cited in Diaz and Berk 1992), for example, points out that private speech and social speech do in fact share important content and structural similarities. As Goudena (1987) suggests, private speech utterances such as 'it doesn't fit' have a clear social nature, as they represent not only a statement about the task, but also a request for adult help.

Another obvious distinction between private speech and social speech is that it has been suggested that speech used by mothers in verbal interaction, perform very similar functions as those performed by children's private speech (Diaz and Berk 1992). Vygotsky (1987) hypothesized that the phenomenon of private speech (self-talk used by children in various situations that is not addressed to others) reflects children's potential for self-direction to plan, guide, and monitor their own goal-directed activity. This can be illustrated in the following example of a 6-year-old girl trying to problem solve a mathematics activity:

> The child is adding two, two-digit numbers: Sarah is at the table and looks at her maths book. She then looks up into the air and begins to quietly count on her

fingers. She stops and pauses and writes something down. She then again looks up in to air and begins to count on her fingers quietly. She then taps her pencil back and forth and looks at her maths paper. She then looks up and observes the child opposite while her lips are moving. She then taps her pencil again and writes the answer down on her paper.

It is clear from this example how Sarah is using private speech utterances, which are personalized to the task she is doing. This includes gestures, movement and observing others. The speech here is not used for the purpose of communication to another peer or adult but as a guiding force in solving the maths problem. According to Vygotsky (1978), the quantity of private speech utterances undertaken by children aged 3–6 years can be linked to their success and task performance.

The relationship between private speech and task performance

A number of researchers, for example Diaz and Berk (1992) and Kohlberg et al. (1968), have investigated this particular aspect, but clear evidence of positive correlation between the frequency of private speech during a given task and task success has been relatively scarce (Berk 1986). Studies utilizing a Vygotskian framework have regularly argued that private speech serves a variety of different functions regarding task performance. These include sustaining attention, guiding problem-solving steps and pacing motor activity. It must also be mentioned that a variable which will affect all of these is task difficulty. Diaz (1992: 76) outlines the relationship between task difficulty and task performance in a four-step progression:

- *Step 1:* If a child is competent in a given task, very little or no use of private speech is necessary.
- *Step 2:* As the task becomes more difficult, challenging the child's current level of ability and competence, private speech will be used in an attempt to gain new and higher levels of mastery on the task.
- *Step 3:* If the child's private speech is in fact sufficient, it will guide and create new and high levels of ability and competence.
- *Step 4:* Finally, increasing levels of competence on the tasks will reduce the need to use private speech bringing the child back gradually to the situation in Step 1.

A study carried out by Zivin (1979) also found that children who were 4 years of age and who did not talk while completing finger mazes were faster and more accurate than children who produced some kind of private speech.

Furthermore, Goodman (1981) reported that even in some studies where there has been some association between private speech and problem solving, task-relevant verbalizations have not necessarily led to more successful task performance. Berk and Landau (1993) claim that the lack of significance between task success and the amount of private speech produced does not necessarily contradict Vygotsky's theory. This is because the amount of private speech invariably increases with difficulty and children are more likely to fail if they find the task too difficult. However, Berk and Landau (1993: 558) conclude that both the production of private speech and the likelihood of failure are 'functions of task difficulty, private speech will more often co-occur with failed tasks that with successful performance'.

There is a notion that private speech can also determine a child's intellectual ability, as it is known to peak earlier for more able children (Kohlberg et al. 1968; Vygotsky 1978). This could be one way in which early years practitioners could observe and assess each child's intellectual capability to inform their future planning. Vygotsky (1978) also observed that the more challenging the task, the more private speech would be produced. In support of this, Levina (1968, cited in Vygotsky 1978) observed that children in an experimental situation not only act in achieving a goal but also speak. Vygotsky concludes from this that private speech (or personalized speech) is as important as the role of action in attaining a goal and that the more complex the task and the less direct its solution, the more there will be an increase in the amount of speech produced (Zivin 1979).

To summarize, the importance of the role of the adult and the dialogues they have with children is paramount for Vygotsky, particularly in relation to adults who engage with the child as a collaborative partner. Vygotsky (1978) argues that children who experience this type of enriched environment are more likely to produce more private speech utterances; they thus master tasks beyond their level more competently and at an earlier stage of their development, emphasizing the importance of the role of the adult in engaging in activities with children including make-believe play, constructive play, outdoor play and more potentially structured activities when private speech (personalized speech) begins at approximately 3 years of age.

The importance of adult–child and child–child dialogue

According to Vygotsky (1978), 'mental functioning in an individual can be understood only by examining the social and cultural processes from which it derives' (Wertsch 1991: 548). Thus to know an individual, we must also understand the social relations in which any particular individual exists by going 'outside' the individual. Bernstein (1996: 21) supports this view and highlights the importance of a child's family and the school, stating, 'the

	School knowledge	Local knowledge
Visible pedagogy	Explicit instruction in the school curriculum (e.g. ABC learned by rote and recited, ABC books taught)	Explicit instruction in a non-school curriculum (e.g. mosque, Sunday school, Urdu classes)
Invisible pedagogy	Implicit instruction in the school curriculum (e.g. fridge magnets, nursery rhyme CDs, DVDs)	Implicit instruction in a non-school curriculum (apprenticeship into home and family routines and responsibilities)

Figure 1.2 An illustration of Bernstein's visible and invisible pedagogy. (Adapted from Brooker 2002: 64)

domestic transmission of school knowledge is more influential in children's subsequent school careers than what is taught and learned' (Bernstein 1996: 21). Bernstein (1996) breaks this down further by referring to school knowledge as 'official' because it is the means of entry into the mainstream culture and local knowledge, which is different for every family and community (illustrated in Figure 1.2).

Moreover, Edmiston (2008: 173) refers to an ethical pedagogy which 'develops from such philosophical assumptions encompasses learning and care and caring within a broad concern of all aspects of life'. Edmiston (2008) then proceeds to argue:

> in using the term pedagogy I reject false dichotomous beliefs that would attempt to separate the social constructivist process of learning from teaching, conceptualise them as divided between adult and child, or view of caring relationships as optional in classrooms.
>
> (Edmiston 2008: 173)

What this suggests is adults albeit at home or in school should be creating a shared culture where children and adults can engage together in a shared dialogue in a potentially wide range of possibilities around 'the locus of an ethical encounter' (Edmiston 2008: 174), where adults and children may collaboratively examine the question of just being together.

Thus, once again highlighting Vygotsky's thinking in relation to the importance of the adult in modelling language, which a child then takes on board when expressing their private speech utterances. Vygotsky's claims about the social origins of mental functioning and the impact of 'going outside' the individual have surfaced in many ways throughout his writings – two issues which have taken a significant importance in his social constructivist approach are public and private speech (as previously mentioned) and the zone of proximal development (Wertsch and Tulviste 1992).

> The ZPD can be defined as the distance between a child's actual development as determined by independent problem solving. The higher level of potential development as determined through problem solving under adult guidance or in collaboration with more capable peers.
>
> (Wertsch and Tulviste 1992: 549)

Vygotsky postulates how the implications of the ZPD are for the observation and assessment of children as well as allowing the teacher to monitor a child's progress and thus to plan a child's next step. This also gives practitioners a baseline to work from for future curriculum planning. Furthermore, as Vygotsky stipulated that practitioners should aim to teach at a child's potential development, he also believed that measuring the child's actual development was important.

The following example illustrates Vygotsky's ideas regarding assessment relating to the ZPD:

> Imagine we have examined two children and have determined that the mental age of both is seven years. This means that both children solve tasks accessible to seven year olds. However when we attempt to push these children further in carrying out the tests, there turns out to be an essential difference between them. With the help of leading questions, examples and demonstrations, one of them easily solves the test items taken from two years above the child's level of (actual) development. The other solves test items that are only a half year above his/her level of (actual) development.
>
> (Vygotsky 1986, cited in Wertsch and Tulviste 1992: 549)

A significant question here relates to whether the development of mental functioning is the same for these two children. In Vygotsky's view they are not the same. This is because, with the help of adults, what a child is capable of doing is acknowledged, hence the child's zone of proximal development. The notion of the ZPD is a key element in the pedagogical approaches to supporting learning as proposed by Vygotsky (1987). Vygotsky illustrates the ZPD with reference to the observation that different children of the same age will be able to achieve tasks of different complexity when tutored by the same adult, 'this difference between the child's actual level of development and actual level of performance that he achieves in collaboration with others, defines the zone of proximal development' (Vygotsky 1987: 209).

Mercer (1991) articulates a neo-Vygotskian perspective in which a practitioner does not treat children's talk as a 'transparent window' on the mind, talk is not 'simply thinking out loud'. Instead the neo-Vygotskian view contends that to talk and to communicate with others through speech is to engage in the 'social nature of thinking' (Mercer 1991: 63). Through talking and listening, information gets shared, people get to know each other, ideas may change and alternative perspectives become available as well as an increase in private speech utterances (Mercer 1991).

Recently in England, longitudinal research in early years settings has identified strong evidence for the value of adults engaging with children collaboratively in activity through the strategy of 'sustained shared thinking' to support their cognitive development (the Effective Provision of Preschool Education (EPPE) Project – Sylva et al. 2004; Researching Effective Pedagogy in the Early Years (REPEY) Project – Siraj-Blatchford et al. 2002). According to Siraj-Blatchford (2007), sustained shared thinking involves

> episodes in which two or more individuals 'worked together' in an intellectual way to solve a problem, clarify a concept, evaluate activities or extend narratives etc. During a period of sustained shared thinking both parties contributed to the thinking and developed and extended the discourse.
>
> (Siraj-Blatchford 2007: 147)

The findings of the EPPE and REPEY projects demonstrate that sustained shared thinking (SST) is crucial for effective, high quality settings.

As Siraj-Blatchford and Manni (2008: 3) note, there are 'strong theoretical resonances' between SST and the work of Vygotsky (1978) in particular in relation to the ZPD. Significantly, the new statutory Early Years Foundation Stage (EYFS) (Department for Education and Skills (DfES) 2007) includes sustained shared thinking as one of its core 'Principles of Learning and Development' (DfES 2007: Sect. 4.3c). All practitioners with young children under 5 in England are therefore currently expected to engage in SST.

As REPEY found, sustained shared thinking was much more likely to happen when children were interacting one to one with an adult or with another child (peer) and that freely chosen play activities often provided the best opportunities for adults to extend children's thinking (Siraj-Blatchford et al. 2002). Based on 'joint activity' (Jordan 2009) involving shared thinking and attention, a child's initiative, participation and influence may be supported, expanded and challenged in different ways and directions. However, there is very limited research evidence to demonstrate exactly how freely chosen (child initiated) play activities afford opportunities for practitioner engagement and SST.

Implications for practice

It is evident in a wide variety of early years settings how influential Vygotsky's thinking has been in changing professional practice, not only in England but across the world. The concept and ideology of the ZPD has arguably become more familiar within the early years workforce; however, Vygotsky's ideas in relation to private speech and how children guide themselves through tasks is less well known. This chapter offers an insight into the concept of private speech and it is argued here that by more closely observing the actions and private speech that children use, practitioners can be provided with an additional understanding of the different ways children accomplish and solve problems and use this understanding to plan and evaluate future activities. With the inclusion of the practice of SST within the EYFS in England, there is an even greater emphasis on practitioners' knowledge of Vygotsky's theory illuminating the role of private or personalized speech.

It follows that pedagogical practices need to provide opportunities for a balance of child and teacher led activities, which are carefully planned and developmentally appropriate through open ended questions and encouraging, engaging and prompting children in internalizing their thoughts through language. Mercer and Littleton (2007) support this view and state that

> we would never claim that everything that can be thought can be thought in language, or that language is involved in all rational thinking. But language is without doubt the most ubiquitous, flexible and creative of the meaning making tools available, and it is the one most intimately connected to the creation and pursuit of reasoned argument.
>
> (Mercer and Littleton 2007: 2)

They therefore argue that language and in particular spoken dialogue deserves special attention and recognition. Mercer and Littleton (2007), highlighting Vygotsky's emphasis on the importance of children learning from the communicative tools and symbols of their culture, remind us that

> social experience does not provide all children with the same language experiences, so we cannot assume that all children naturally have access to the same opportunities for developing their use of language as a tool for learning, reasoning and solving problems.
>
> (Mercer and Littleton 2007: 2)

Thus children without the good practice of modelling and the guidance of a practitioner may not gain access to some very useful ways of 'using language as a tool for reasoning, learning and working collaboratively because those "ways with words" are simply not part of their experience' (Mercer and Littleton 2007: 3).

In England current government initiated projects such as 'I Can' (2008) and 'Every Child a Talker' (National Strategies Early Years 2008)) are aimed at raising the awareness of parents and practitioners with regard to the importance of speech, language and communication for children in their earliest years. As this chapter has illustrated, children who engage in enriched language environments are more likely to produce more private speech utterances and master tasks above their current level of development. As Vygotsky (1978: 7) stated, 'the mechanism of individual developmental change is rooted in a child's society and culture'.

Suggested further reading

Daniels, H. (2001) *Vygotsky and Pedagogy*. London: Routledge.
Kozulin, A., Ginis, B., Ageyey, V.S. and Miller, S.M. (2003) *Vygotsky's Educational Theory in Cultural Context*. New York: Cambridge University Press.
Mercer, N. and Littleton, K. (2007) *Dialogue and the Development of Children's Thinking*. London: Routledge.

References

Berk, L.E. (1986) 'Relationship of elementary school children's private speech to behavioural accompaniment to ask, attention and task performance.' *Development Psychology*, 22(5): 671–680.
Berk, L.E. (1992) 'Children's private speech: A overview of theory and the status of research.' In R.M. Diaz and L.E. Berk (eds) *Private Speech: From social interaction to self regulation*. Hillsdale, NJ: Lawrence Erlbaum Associates.
Berk, L.E. and Garvin, R.A. (1984) 'Development of private speech among low income Appalachian children'. *Developmental Psychology*, 20(2): 271–286.
Berk, L.E. and Landau, S. (1993) 'Private speech of learning disabled and normally achieving children in classroom and laboratory contexts.' *Child Development*, 64: 556–571.
Bernstein, B. (1996) *Pedagogy, Symbolic Control, and Identity*. London: Taylor & Francis.
Bivens, J.A. and Berk, L.E. (1990) 'A longitudinal study of elementary school children's private speech.' *Merrill Palmer Quarterly*, 36(4): 443–463.
Brooker, L. (2002) *Starting School: Young children learning cultures*. Buckingham: Open University Press.
Daniels, H. (2001) *Vygotsky and Pedagogy*. London: RoutledgeFalmer.

Davydov, V.D. and Zinchenko, V.P. (1989) 'Vygotsky's contribution to the development of psychology.' *Soviet Psychology*, 27(2): 22–36.

Department for Education and Skills (DfES) (2007) *The Early Years Foundation Stage: Setting the standards for learning, development and care*. Nottingham: DfES.

Diaz, R. (1992) 'Methodological concerns in the study of private speech.' In R.M. Diaz and L.E. Berk (eds) *Private Speech: From social interaction to self regulation*. Hillsdale, NJ: Lawrence Erlbaum Associates.

Diaz, R.M. and Berk, L.E. (eds) (1992) *Private Speech: From social interaction to self regulation*. Hillsdale, NJ: Lawrence Erlbaum Associates.

Driscoll, P.M. (2000) *Psychology of Learning for Instruction*. Boston, MA: Allyn & Bacon.

Edmiston, B. (2008) *Forming Ethical Identities in Early Childhood Play*. London: Routledge.

Fernyhough, C. and Lloyd, P. (1999) *Lev Vygtosky: Critical assessments*. New York: Routledge.

Goodman, S.H. (1981) 'The integration of verbal and motor behaviour in preschool children.' *Child Development*, 52: 280–289.

Goudena, P.P. (1987) 'The social nature of private speech of preschoolers during problem solving.' *International Journal of Behavioral Development*, 10: 187–206.

I Can (2008) *I Can Early Talk: A supportive service for children's communication. Accreditation standards*. Available at www.ican.org.uk/early%20talk/accreditation%20information/communication%20settings.aspx (accessed 14 September 2009).

Jordan, B. (2009) 'Scaffolding learning and co-constructing understandings.' In A. Anning, J. Cullen and M. Fleer (eds) *Early Childhood Education*, 2nd edn. London: Sage.

Kohlberg, L., Yaeger, J. and Hjerthol, E. (1968) 'Private speech: Four studies and a review of theories.' *Child Development*, 39: 691–736.

Kozulin, A., Gindis, B., Ageyey, S.A. and Miller, S.M. (2003) *Vygotsky's Educational Theory in Cultural Context*. New York: Cambridge University Press.

Mead, G.H. (1934) *Mind, Self and Society*. Chicago, IL: University of Chicago Press.

Mercer, N. (1991) 'Accounting for what goes on in classrooms: What have neo-Vygotskians got to offer?' *Education Section Review*, 15(2): 61–67.

Mercer, N. and Littleton, K. (2007) *Dialogue and the Development of Children's Thinking*. Abingdon: Routledge.

National Strategies Early Years (2008) *Every Child a Talker: Guidance for early language lead practitioners*. Nottingham: DCSF.

Piaget, J. (1929) *The Child's Conception of the World*. London: Routledge.

Piaget, J. (1953) 'How children form mathematical concepts.' *Scientific American*, November: 74–79.

Siraj-Blatchford, I. (2007) 'Creativity, communication and collaboration: The identification of pedagogical progression in sustained shared thinking.' *Asia Pacific Journal of Research in Early Childhood*, 1(2): 99–114.

Siraj-Blatchford, I., Sylva, K., Muttock, S., Gilden, R. and Bell, D. (2002) *Researching Effective Pedagogy in the Early Years*. Research Report 356. Oxford: Department of Educational Studies, University of Oxford.

Siraj-Blatchford, I. and Manni, L. (2008) '"Would you like to tidy up now?" An analysis of adult questioning in the English Foundation Stage.' *Early Years: An International Journal of Research and Development*, 28(1): 5–22.

Smith, P., Cowie, H. and Blades, M. (1998) *Understanding Children's Development*, 3rd edn. Oxford: Blackwell.

Stone, A. (1998) 'The metaphor of scaffolding: Its utility for the field of learning disabilities.' *Journal of Learning Disabilities*, 3(4): 344–364.

Sylva, K., Melhuish, E., Sammons, P., Siraj-Blatchford, I. and Taggart, B. (2004) *The Effective Provision of Pre-school Education (EPPE) Project: Findings from preschool to the end of Key Stage 1*. London: Institute of Education, University of London.

Vygotsky, L.S. (1978) *Mind in Society: The development of higher psychological processes*. Cambridge, MA: Harvard University Press.

Vygotsky, L.S. (1987) *The Collected Works of L.S. Vygotsky, Volume 1*. New York: Plenum.

Wells, G. (1999) *Dialogic Enquiry: Toward a sociocultural practice and theory of education*. Cambridge: Cambridge University Press.

Wertsch, J.V. (1979) 'From social interaction to higher psychological processes: A clarification and application of Vygotsky's theory.' *Human Development*, 22: 1–22.

Wertsch, J.V. (1991) *Voices of the Mind: A sociocultural approach to mediated action*. Hemel Hempstead: Harvester Wheatsheaf.

Wertsch, J.V. and Tulviste, P. (1992) 'L.S. Vygotsky and contemporary developmental psychology.' *Developmental Psychology*, 28(4): 548–557.

Zivin, G. (1979) *Removing Common Confusions about Egocentric Speech and Self Regulation*. New York: Wiley.

2 Bruner: the power of story and identity

Lynn Richards

Born in New York in 1915, Jerome S. Bruner began his career as an academic psychologist at Harvard. Turning his attention to issues of education in the 1950s, he initiated what was to become a lifelong passion for the topics of pedagogy, schooling, thinking and learning. Bruner took up the position of Watts Professor of Psychology at Oxford in 1972 and continued to research and publish widely in the domain of early cognitive development and preschool education. Seeking to improve the life chances of young children within Head Start, the Pre-School Playgroup Association, and as a consultant to the preschools of Reggio Emilia, Bruner's influence has been to continually search for new possibilities within education. Bruner is now back in his native New York and works as a university professor at the School of Law.

Introduction

This chapter introduces the reader to some of the powerful ideas of Bruner, who, as an eminent American psychologist, has enthralled audiences for decades with his profound erudition and his engaging and playful style of delivery. Indeed, I had the privilege of hearing him speak at a public lecture in Oxford in 2007, where I was struck by his indomitable belief in the content of his speech, entitled 'Cultivating the Possible' (Bruner 2007); now in his nineties, Bruner continues to push the boundaries of what might be possible. As illustrative of his own philosophy on the nature of education, Bruner places a high significance on the power of language to transform schooling practices and his memories of his teacher, Miss Orcutt, as 'a rarity...a human event not a transmission device' (Bruner 1986: 26) exemplify the values of dialogue and negotiation on the young mind. For Bruner (2006: 171), '[p]edagogy is never innocent. It is a medium that carries its own message' and this chapter seeks to stimulate discussion of how practitioners and students might usefully wish to reflect upon their own, and others', use of language in their work with young children and their families.

As if reflected in his own communicative skills, the *search for meaning*, as a product of language, is a central tenet of Bruner's work and provides the main topic of exploration for this chapter. The power of words to construct social realities and the potential of culture to control meaning, through the socially accepted and desirable communal ways of thinking and valuing, will be examined. The place of narrative as a mode of thought is a key concept in Bruner's writings and will be explored here in terms of its impact on ways of thinking about the human condition and its ability to explicate meaning (Bruner 1990: 96), in particular, its ability to shape and determine life stories (Bruner 2006: 131). In pursuance of this, and as a way of demonstrating the impact of Bruner's ideas on my own research interests, within the field of race, this chapter also seeks to uncover the power of language to influence identity formation.

Language is a powerful symbolic tool. It allows us, as humans, to interact and to connect with each other in a meaningful way and yet knowing the etiquette for interaction is key to acceptance within the social cut-and-thrust of human exchange. I first became interested in the power of everyday speech having viewed a television programme entitled *Teenage Tourette's Camp* (ITV 1 2006). The programme detailed the difficulties of a small percentage of young people with Tourette's Syndrome who demonstrated the rather unnerving condition of 'coprolalia'; this syndrome manifested itself in the involuntary symptom of shouting out swear words and 'ethnic slurs' – in this case, the word 'nigger'. On the one hand, the young people violated the conventional rules of exchange by shouting out obscenities in a quite unexpected manner; on the other hand, the word 'nigger' is one that would seem to have belonged to a past era and not one I would have associated with these young people. In an age when 'political correctness' seeks, rightly, to constrain the impulses of prejudice and discrimination, I became intrigued by the potential of everyday speech to harbour thoughts and feelings that may lie beneath the overtly expressed words. My interest led me to carry out a small-scale research study involving the voices of early years student-practitioners and their perceptions of race. The work of Bruner helped me to uncover the mechanisms of human interaction and to view the voices of the research participants as representative of a dominant cultural backdrop:

> When we enter human life, it is as if we walk on stage into a play whose enactment is already in progress – a play whose somewhat open plot determines what parts we may play and toward what de-nouements we may be heading.
>
> (Bruner 1990: 34)

A passion for the ordinary

For Bruner, psychology is required to offer a systematic description and explanation of ordinary behaviour. The positivist quest for scientific 'truth' and the behaviourism of the mid-twentieth century are witnessed in his work (Bruner 2006) but are a far cry from the more purposive study of meaning-making that Bruner later sought within the cognitive revolution of the 1970s, and which he proposes as a 'central process of a cultural psychology' (Bruner 1990: 64). He argues the presence of two modes of thought which serve to order human experience; the paradigmatic, driven by a search for objectivity and logical truth, and the narrative, driven by a search for the meaning of experience within human intentions. In order to give structure to his thinking, Bruner draws heavily on the study of linguistics which he admires not only for its ability to 'look at natural, ordinary behaviour – speaking or comprehending ordinary speech – but for its aim of describing the banal and the ordinary systematically' (Bruner 2006: 44). Indeed, it is this passion for the ordinary which illuminates Bruner's work that influences my own interest in him. As someone who is seeking to uncover what might be an underlying racial script within the day-to-day exchanges of ordinary workers within the field of early years practice, it is this systematic observation and analysis of language that holds my fascination.

The underpinning rules and protocols for speaking and comprehending are exhaustively reviewed by Bruner as a way of laying bare the implicit conventions of an entire language system. The capacity for language to transmit meaning is seen to rely on a mutual understanding between the person delivering the words and the person receiving them; such an understanding is not premised on the content alone, but on the processes by which it is formulated and interpreted. The work of Ferdinand de Saussure (1916, cited in Culler 1976: 22), within the field of linguistics and semiology, is drawn upon here to acknowledge the uniqueness of relational properties that exist between what he terms the 'signifier' and the 'signified': 'Each language articulates or organizes the world differently.' In addition, the context in which the exchange is made has a key role to play in determining the intended, and received, meaning. It becomes evident, then, that the conventional maxims must be known and appreciated for the exchange to have understanding for both parties. Such an understanding, however, would not appear to be as straightforward as it might first appear. Bernstein (1971: 220), for instance, emphasizes the significance of 'context' when exploring notions of 'elaborated' and 'restricted' linguistic codes, and concludes that the 'social classes differ in terms of the *contexts* which evoke certain linguistic realizations'. For Bernstein, socialization processes of young children – couched within particular linguistic codes – will determine levels of success in wider societal contexts, such as schooling, so that mutual understanding of conventional maxims may often be wrongly assumed.

Mutual understanding may be furnished by the backdrop of a broader structure and, for Bruner, this is provided by culture. The values and beliefs of an entire community, society or, indeed, nation, constitute the means by which culture is formulated and against which meanings are shared and understood; culture becomes, then, a sort of dictionary that arbitrates meaning, although the 'symbolic capital' outlined by Bourdieu (1991: 72), in terms of linguistic efficacy, would stress the power differentials between individuals, and the social conditions in question. Having an appreciation, then, of shared cultural meaning is of prime importance in being able to participate in the linguistic codes and constructions that are embodied within the shared language; not only the meaning of the words as understood within the cultural interpretation but also the whole mechanism of making sense of what has been said, and in what context. Notions such as these find resonance in the work of Donaldson (1978) who, in expounding the significance of contextualized speech and its cultural interpretations, cites the example of a North American Indian (sic) who was unable to translate the sentence 'The white man shot six bears today' into his native language. When asked why this proved problematic, the translator noted unequivocally that 'No white man could shoot six bears in one day!' (Donaldson 1978: 38). The context, and what Bruner would refer to as 'canonical images' (those embedded ways of thinking, being and acting) of a culture, determine what is possible and this example testifies perhaps to the power of culture to control meaning, and indeed, to limit possible understandings.

My research study

In my own research, the background structure within which I worked was represented by the culture of whiteness. Looking to examine the conversational speech of white student-practitioners, the arbiter of meanings became the shared cultural norms and those 'canonical images' to do with thinking, being, and acting within whiteness. There is a raft of literature on the topic which offers the overwhelming attribute of whiteness to be its sense of neutrality and invisibility (Frankenberg 1993; Dyer 1997; Kincheloe et al. 1998; Levine-Rasky 2000; Pearce 2005); that is, its ability to 'be there' without ever being noticed, as the metaphorical elephant in the living room (Gaine 2005: 24). While on the one hand it encompasses a set of physical and physiological traits, it is also perceived as a set of behaviours which although 'invisible to whites [is] hypervisible to people of color' (sic) (Rasmussen et al. 2001: 10). The 'canonical images' of whiteness then become those attributes of power and privilege which do not require justification or defence.

My research study sought to uncover embedded racial scripts, or narratives, that played themselves out in a daily exchange of expression, and reinforcement by others. The very nature of the subject matter, together with a desire for the 'researcher–researched relationship' to be made as equitable as possible, located this collection of qualitative data within a poststructuralist approach, where the significance of meaning, power and identity were readily apparent (Hughes 2001). Focus groups were used as the data collection instrument since they provide an opportunity for the expression of ideas which are seldom mentioned in everyday context (Farquhar 1999). Stratified sampling was used to form two focus groups; diversity was established across groups, characterized by age of participant and length of experience within an early childhood setting, while 'homogeneity' was targeted within groups to facilitate greater commonality for shared meaning (Fern 2001). All focus group participants were female. The human desire to find meaning, and indeed to sustain culturally shared norms, seemed to follow very much the arguments expounded by Bruner, with dominant narratives as the cohesive mechanism

Linguistic devices

As a part of that cohesive force, the conventional rules that underpin communication (pragmatics) are seen to also include a range of linguistic devices that can greatly influence, and so disrupt, the meaning of the words delivered and their intended interpretation; such devices as speech acts, conversational implicatures and triggering of presuppositions (Bruner 2006: 122). It is argued that the refined use of such devices is absorbed early in the life of the child so that linguistic conventions are shared by members of a community and their use depends on the ability of knowing that others will understand them too. In this way, a 'spectrum of possible meanings' (Bruner 1986: 25) becomes apparent and is reflective of the narrative mode of thought which deals in the expression of human mental states, inclusive of uncertainty, and of implicit rather than explicit meanings. So, the way in which words are used in human interaction may convey more than the individual meaning of the words used, or indeed may mean something quite different to those used. Within the literature on whiteness, this notion is evidenced in the work of Sleeter (1996), who argues that the boundaries of whiteness are patrolled by members of the group themselves to maintain race solidarity, and this may be done by 'racial bonding' and the use of 'codewords' (Sleeter 1996: 261). In addition, Sleeter (1996) is supported by Hurtado (1999: 234), who suggests that the 'power solidarity' of whiteness is socialized 'in the intimacy of families', where privilege depends on members not betraying unspoken power dynamics. Such ways of talking and comprehending represent what McLaren (1998) refers to as 'unmarked practices' which allow the centrality of whiteness, and so its invisibility, as a position of privilege to continue unexamined, and so unchallenged.

As a way of endeavouring to provide an example of such linguistic devices, the following conversation is offered; the dialogue would seem to bear witness to a process of 'meaning-making' whereby underlying beliefs and values are played out when considering the extent to which the UK is a tolerant nation:

Student 1:   I think we're very tolerant now, I think we've flipped over perhaps, even gone...

Student 2:   Do you think we're...we're too tolerant?

Student 1:   I don't know too tolerant

Student 2:   Embracing other cult...cultures

Student 1:   I think it'd be...we're a flagship, and I think it'd be really nice if...if in a spirit of do unto others as they do unto you, if everybody did the same, it'd be good. But at the moment we seem to be the only ones that are really up there doing it. We're like a beacon of how it should be done, sort of thing.

Researcher: Do you mean as a country?

Student 1:   Yeah! I do actually, I do. I think that we really do embrace and our policies are all there and.....there's laws now in this country and you...they're being perhaps not upheld in every case, but everyone knows about them now and so we're very accepting and tolerant people really. It just shows when you queue up and you go on holiday really...

The parting comment here would seem to testify to a 'hidden narrative' (Cohen 1992) of 'judgement'; in this case, the unspoken frustration with those who do not know that it is polite to form an orderly queue, with its implicit links to feelings of superiority. There is also a strong Christian lexis in the remark with its inclusion of 'do unto others...' which finds echoes in Bonnett's (2000) association with whiteness. The remark was not taken up by other participants and may identify an instance of 'white racial bonding' (Sleeter 1996: 261) where tacit agreement with a racial world view serves to maintain race solidarity. The requirement, therefore, to be a fully paid-up member of the cultural group is key to establishing, and maintaining, a shared context of meaning.

The narrative device

The way in which language is used provides a focal point for Bruner's thinking and he explores in detail the linguistic devices that are to be found in everyday parlance. In keeping with his focus on the 'ordinary', it is noted that adherence to conversational maxims can result in exchanges that are dull and flat so that a breaking of the rules can initiate greater demands on the role of the interpreter, creating the potential for new meanings. For Bruner, this is represented by the narrative mode, which he describes as both 'utterance' as well as written format, but which is exhaustively connected to the writing of stories. The ability to generate ambiguity is seen as a helpful way to engage the person receiving the message. It is the reader as part of the composition that is encouraged, a sort of 'filler-in' of gaps, which lends itself to this style of writing, premised on devices which leave open and uncertain the specific meaning of a text. In storytelling, Bruner is emphatic that this is indeed the way to excite and motivate readers and listeners, in stark contrast to the flat delivery when keeping strictly to the conventional maxims of exchange; here Bruner draws heavily on the work of the Russian linguist, Jakobson, who encouraged writers to "make it strange' to overcome automatic writing (Bruner 1986: 22). Indeed, Bruner argues that this is a device to actively engage the reader as 'complicitous with the characters in the exchange' (Bruner 1986: 27) and although this can create what he terms 'narrative tension' within a story, the notion finds a more menacing resonance in my own research on whiteness.

Levine-Rasky (2000) argues that the structural advantages of whiteness mean that the holder of privilege is oblivious to the effects of oppression, so that the implicit option is to ignore it. Meanwhile, however, the material and psychological gains offered to fully paid-up members infer there is 'tacit agreement to continue to reap the benefits' (Sleeter 1996: 259) which, in turn, legitimizes the existing structural order in a way that seeks to evade complicity in any inequality. So, while the narrative mode for Bruner encourages ambiguity – offering the opportunity for complicity as part of the storytelling toolkit – within the banality of everyday conversational exchange, ambiguity can be a means whereby some are excluded from the talk; coded ways of speaking and listening may serve to shore up membership of a particular grouping, so isolating others. A further example from my own study seeks to explain this more fully:

Student 2:   No one can say no! You can't do that. And I think that's possibly an aspect of the culture that attracts people ... particularly from a very narrow culture that doesn't have those openings for you to be able to change how you live perhaps.

Later in the group discussion, it became apparent that Islam was the 'narrow culture' within this particular focus group; an example perhaps of Sleeter's (1996: 261) use of 'codewords', and a way in which the words alone could not reveal their intended meaning without an implicit, or tacit, understanding of the context in operation. The power of words to constitute meaning and to

transmit cultural understanding in shared stories and life narratives has reper-
cussions for those who may not be considered a part of that shared cultural
heritage.

Meaning-making

The narrative mode of thought is integral to Bruner's understanding of how
the lived experience is organized and interpreted. The young child's propen-
sity for storytelling is not seen as merely a coincidence but as a result of a
culture's way of predisposing the child to become familiar with its ways of
being, thinking, and acting: 'our capacity to render experience in terms of
narrative is not just child's play, but an instrument for making meaning that
dominates much of life in culture – from soliloquies at bedtime to the weigh-
ing of testimony in our legal system' (Bruner 1990: 96). The predominance
of these underlying narratives constitute a sort of culturally endorsed landscape across which individuals navigate their life journeys in keeping with
the extant narrative models available. In this way, culture is transmitted in-
tergenerationally, in true Vygotskian (1978) style, determining not only how
life is, but also how it should be.

In my own research, I was seeking to illuminate those underlying narratives of race that, as part of the cultural fabric of whiteness, socialized
in the early years of life, continued to guide the thinking of these student-
practitioners. Bruner identifies how the power of one narrative over another
has the potential to establish hegemonic control, as well as determining ideas
of selfhood (Bruner 1990: 114). In pursuance of this, a further example is
offered here, drawn from my research study: the one participant shows an
extensive knowledge of Hindu and Muslim faiths and lifestyles, and ostensi-
bly appears to work actively to promote equitable practice within her early
years setting. However, her articulated words would seem to demonstrate an
underlying racial narrative of superiority and 'knowing better':

Student 1:   One in particular...erm, Muslim family and they use the ex-
             cuse of Eid for everything (...) 'cos they think there's a lack of
             knowledge on our part and that we don't know the dates of
             things...Little things like that...well, actually it's not Eid for
             another couple of days...and well, now think of something.

The student-practitioner gives the impression of not wishing to be 'caught
out' by a lack of knowledge, so undermining her own authority; the infer-
ence that the family would need an excuse demonstrates an unequal partnership, based perhaps on perceived assumptions of difference. Such an account
finds echoes in the work of Frankenberg (1993: 143), who refers to 'selective

engagement with difference' which, while seeking to embrace cultural parameters, leaves hierarchies intact and so 'leads white women back into complicity with structural and institutional dimensions of inequality'. This example
would seem to illustrate the power of language, as a constituent of social reality, to determine thinking and behaving, despite personal endeavours to
move away from those 'canonical images' embedded within the very fabric
of cultural reference. Such a limitation of language to express human mental
intentions is encapsulated in what McLaren (1998) terms the inadequacy of
'semantic availability' when attempting to move out of the binary stance of
whiteness.

The power of narrative

The ability to negotiate new meanings and understandings is seen by Bruner
to reside in the collaborative act of dialogue, where the narrative mode has the
power to bring together both the canonical and the exceptional; indeed, it is
within such narrative mode that 'cultivating the possible' is to be found. This
viewpoint is not new to his writing; in 1990 he writes: 'the viability of a culture inheres in its capacity for resolving conflicts, for explicating differences
and renegotiating communal meanings' (Bruner 1990: 47). The mass movement of peoples from one continent to another, and the resultant changes in
population diversity within the UK alone, raises problems for social inclusion
if a culture's 'canonical ways' are immovable. The meeting of minds, with
their inherent ways of thinking, being, and acting, necessitates shifts in the
'canonical images' so that judgements are made on the basis of changing values and beliefs; in other words, the stories embedded within the culture need
to change, to encompass new ways of being, thinking, and acting that can be
woven into the culture's fabric of 'what is' and 'what should be'.

    The ability and power of language to construct social realities – to do
with identity and race – impact greatly on the lived experiences of us all.
Bruner is not the only writer to appreciate the importance of stories; for instance Stainton-Rogers and Stainton-Rogers (1992: 6–7, cited in Prout 2005:
56) note emphatically: 'The basic thesis . . . is very simple. We live in a world
that is produced through stories – stories we are told, stories that we recount
and stories that we create'. In a racially and ethnically diverse society, it is
imperative that all of us are able to find ourselves in the culturally accepted
stories of the day. In a chapter entitled 'Life as narrative', Bruner (2006: 131)
argues that the stories we tell ourselves 'come to take control of our ways of
life'. In this way, individuals are shaped and afforded value by the culture's
stories; absence from them, or the influence of negative stories, necessarily
impacts on personal identity-forming processes. However, in the UK where
more diverse lifestyles are finding expression as a result of immigration, as

well as more fluid working conditions engendered throughout the European Union, it is perhaps difficult to concede that such stories can keep apace with the variety of cultural narratives represented. In further consideration of the power of narrative to determine life stories, Bruner (1986) comments:

> For stories define the range of canonical characters, the settings in which they operate, the actions that are permissible and comprehensible. And thereby they provide, so to speak, a map of possible roles and of possible worlds in which action, thought and self-definition are permissible (or desirable).
>
> (Bruner 1986: 66)

In terms of diversity, as expressed within notions of race and ethnicity, it is pertinent to consider those 'canonical images' that already exist within the cultural stories on offer. To return, for a final time, to my research study, there follows an example perhaps of one such version; student-practitioners are talking of their perceptions of Asian people:

Student 4: . . . A stereotype of them is they are . . . . they own a shop on the corner . . . It is though, isn't it? When you go into school you always say the Paki shop.
Student 5: Yeah! . . . You do. It's the truth.
Student 6: No! I've never said that.
Student 5: I've heard people say it.
Student 4: Yeah! . . . It's just an automatic thing. You automatically think that if . . . [conversation continues]

It is interesting in this exchange to note the dissent that is offered by Student 6. Earlier on during the focus group meeting, this student had declared herself to be of 'mixed race', that is, having one white parent and one black parent. During this exchange she asserts her independence and disassociates herself from the implied racism of what might be determined as part of a 'canonical image' within this particular storyline. Student 5 then becomes quick to distance herself from the overtly racist comment despite having been in agreement just a few moments previously. In explanation of this, Schick (2000: 96) might suggest that such a repositioning testifies to an attempt to maintain her own 'white liberalist position' in the face of challenge to the perceived narrative. It is noteworthy also that, in this instance, what might be termed 'boundary maintenance' around the parameters of whiteness is ensured by Student 4's use of the word 'automatically', with its overtones of normality and racial licence (Schick 2000: 84), while repetition of the word serves to re-establish race solidarity by means of 'racial bonding' (Sleeter 1996: 261); the threat of the mixed race student-practitioner to disrupt the 'canonical images' of the culturally accepted narrative is acknowledged and action is immediately taken to effect damage limitation. The conversation moves on without bearing witness to the opportunity for fuller dialogue and discussion regarding the seemingly overt measures to 'close ranks'; 'cultivating the possible', then, may require more than words alone.

Schooling

For Bruner, 'education is a complex pursuit of fitting a culture to the needs of its members and of fitting its members and their ways of knowing to the needs of the culture' (Bruner 1996: 42). This marks an important aspect in the formation of identity and Bruner is keen to emphasize that if young people are unable to find their own place within the accepted narratives of a culture, then what follows can be alienation and disaffection. The opportunity to renegotiate meaning is part of Bruner's 'culture-making' and is based on the social constructivist ideals of dialogue and discussion; he is emphatic that such ideals allow for democratic processes to accommodate the changing nature of modern lives (Bruner 1990: 30). Such a perspective is fervently upheld by Alexander (2006: 36), who actively promotes the need for dialogue within school classrooms as a way of countering unquestioned social orders within contemporary society: '[i]t is clear already that a dialogic pedagogy does not sit comfortably with a rigidly canonical – that is to say, monologic – account of knowledge'. In terms of my research study, such an unquestioned social order would be representative of whiteness, so the opportunities to discuss issues of race within the classroom would offer, I would argue, a powerful way forward in allowing children and young people to 'unpack' prevailing narratives. This idea would find favour with Bruner since he specifically advocates that 'a curriculum ought to be built around the great issues, principles, and values that a society deems worthy of the continual concern of its members' (Bruner 1960/1977: 52). However, since language is constitutive of reality, the opportunity to renegotiate meanings within the classroom requires openness on the part of practitioners, as well as an awareness of how language itself may seek to evade such transformative processes.

The work of Pearce (2005) looks at working as a white teacher in a multiethnic school and charts the progress of her own observations in relation to whiteness impacting on her behaviour within the classroom. She argues that talking race is an unfamiliar topic for many white teachers and the fear of saying the wrong thing can be a severely inhibiting factor (Pearce 2003, 2005). This has huge implications for 'cultivating the possible' within schools in the UK where the majority of teachers may hold race narratives embedded with 'canonical images' of whiteness. In order to reach those 'possible worlds' where meaning becomes blurred and so in need of interpretation, with the active participation of those involved, Bruner (2006: 181) cites the example of Paley (1992), whose *You Can't Say You Can't Play* uses storytelling to promote concepts of equality and compassion within the kindergarten classroom. The stories of Magpie use metaphor – couched within narrative mode – to show ways of thinking, being, and acting that young children are encouraged to discuss, and to emulate. Paley emphasizes that it is 'the *habit* of exclusion that grows strong; the identity of those being excluded is not a major obstacle' (Paley 1992: 117) and this finds echoes in the words of Bruner (1996: 24) in acknowledging the profound influence of the classroom upon children's personal narratives, and later life chances. The opportunity for dialogue and negotiation within the classroom is instrumental to Bruner's thinking and he resolutely advocates that teachers, as 'ultimate change agents' (Bruner 1996: 84) can provide opportunities for transformative learning to 'cultivate the possible', just as his own teacher, Miss Orcutt, had done when 'negotiating the world of wonder and possibility' (Bruner 1986: 126) in her class of 10-year-olds.

Conclusion

This chapter has sought to explore the power of words to frame experience and give meaning to life stories within the embedded – 'canonical' – narrative models available within a cultural landscape. The constraints of language, however, can be seen to have limiting effects; as social realities are constituted by language itself, so the need for renegotiation of what constitutes acceptable and desirable narrative models becomes problematic. Against the cultural backdrop of whiteness, I have argued that linguistic devices may serve to shore up hegemonic positioning of power and privilege, so that individuals may find themselves trapped in McLaren's (1998) notion of 'semantic availability' whereby the desire to negotiate new meanings and understandings is compromised by the constitutive power of language itself. Bruner's affirmation, noted earlier, of the claim by Jakobson for writers to "make it strange' to overcome automatic writing (Bruner 1986: 22) finds resonance in the work of Dyer (1997: 10) who declares that in order to move forward in terms of affording value to individual identities 'whiteness needs to be made strange'.

Suggested further reading

Hooks, b. (1994) *Teaching to Transgress: Education as the practice of freedom.* London: Routledge.

Paley, V.G. (1992) *You Can't Say You Can't Play.* Cambridge, MA: Harvard University Press.

Pearce, S. (2005) *You Wouldn't Understand: White teachers in multiethnic classrooms.* Stoke-on-Trent: Trentham Books.

References

Alexander, R. (2006) *Towards Dialogic Teaching: Rethinking classroom talk*, 3rd edn. Cambridge: Dialogos.

Bernstein, B. (1971) *Class, Codes and Control*. St Albans: Granada (published in 1973 by Paladin).

Bonnett, A. (2000) *White Identities: Historical and international perspectives*. Harlow: Prentice Hall/Pearson Education.

Bourdieu, P. (1991) *Language and Symbolic Power*. Cambridge: Polity.

Bruner, J.S. (1960/1977) *The Process of Education*. Cambridge, MA: Harvard University Press.

Bruner, J.S. (1986) *Actual Minds, Possible Worlds*. Cambridge, MA: Harvard University Press.

Bruner, J.S. (1990) *Acts of Meaning*. Cambridge, MA: Harvard University Press.

Bruner, J.S. (1996) *The Culture of Education*. Cambridge, MA: Harvard University Press.

Bruner, J.S. (2006) *In Search of Pedagogy, Volume 2*. London: Routledge.

Bruner, J.S. (2007) 'Cultivating the Possible.' Public lecture, University of Oxford, 13 March. No printed paper issued. Available at www.edstud.ox.ac.uk/about/webcast.html (accessed 26 May 2007).

Cohen, P. (1992) ' "It's racism what dunnit": Hidden narratives in theories of racism.' In J. Donald and A. Rattansi (eds) *'Race', Culture and Difference*. London: Sage.

Culler, J. (1976) *Saussure*. Glasgow: Fontana.

Donaldson, M. (1978) *Children's Minds*. London: Fontana.

Dyer, R. (1997) *White*. London: Routledge.

Farquhar, C. (with Das, R.) (1999) 'Are focus groups suitable for "sensitive" topics?' In R.S. Barbour and J. Kitzinger (eds) *Developing Focus Group Research: Politics, theory and practice*. London: Sage.

Fern, E.F. (2001) *Advanced Focus Group Research*. London: Sage.

Frankenberg, R. (1993) *White Women, Race Matters: The social construction of whiteness*. London: Routledge.

Gaine, C. (2005) *We're All White, Thanks: The persisting myth about 'white' schools*. Stoke-on-Trent: Trentham Books.

Hughes, P. (2001) 'Paradigms, methods and knowledge.' In G. MacNaughton, S.A. Rolfe and I. Siraj-Blatchford (eds) *Doing Early Childhood Research: International perspectives on theory and practice*. Maidenhead: Open University Press.

Hurtado, A. da (1999) 'The trickster's play: Whiteness in the subordination and liberation process.' In R.D. Torres, L.F. Miron and J.X. Inda (eds) *Race, Identity, and Citizenship: A reader*. Oxford: Blackwell.

ITV 1 (2006) *Teenage Tourette's Camp*. ITV Television, 3 January 2006, 9.00 p.m.

Kincheloe, J.L., Steinberg, S.R., Rodriguez, N.M. and Chennault, R.E. (eds) (1998) *White Reign: Deploying whiteness in America*. New York: St Martin's Griffin.

Levine-Rasky, C. (2000) 'Framing whiteness: Working through the tensions in introducing whiteness to educators.' *Race Ethnicity and Education*, 3(3): 271–292.

McLaren, P. (1998) 'Whiteness is . . . The struggle for postcolonial hybridity.' In J.L. Kincheloe, S.R. Steinberg, N.M. Rodriguez and R.E. Chennault (eds) *White Reign: Deploying whiteness in America*. New York: St Martin's Griffin.

Paley, V.G. (1992) *You Can't Say You Can't Play*. Cambridge, MA: Harvard University Press.

Pearce, S. (2003) 'Compiling the White Inventory: The practice of whiteness in a British primary school.' *Cambridge Journal of Education*, 33(2): 273–287.

Pearce, S. (2005) *You Wouldn't Understand: White teachers in multiethnic classrooms*. Stoke-on-Trent: Trentham Books.

Prout, A. (2005) *The Future of Childhood*. Abingdon: RoutledgeFalmer.

Rasmussen, B.B., Klinenberg, E., Nexica, I.J. and Wray, M. (eds) (2001) *The Making and Unmaking of Whiteness*. Durham, NC: Duke University Press.

Saussure, F. de (1916) *Cours de linguistique générale* (published in UK in 1983 as *The Course in General Linguistics*). London: Duckworth.

Schick, C. (2000) ' "By virtue of being white": Resistance in anti-racist pedagogy.' *Race Ethnicity and Education*, 3(1): 83–102.

Sleeter, C.E. (1996) 'White silence, White solidarity.' In N. Ignatiev and J. Garvey (eds) *Race Traitor*. London: Routledge.

Stainton-Rogers, R. and Stainton-Rogers, W. (1992) *Stories of Childhood: Shifting agendas of child concern*. Hemel Hempstead: Harvester Wheatsheaf.

Vygotsky, L.S. (1978) *Mind in Society: The development of higher psychological processes*. Cambridge, MA: Harvard University Press.

3 Howard Gardner's multiple intelligences: every child a learner

Sue Fawson and Gill Woods

Howard Gardner is a renowned developmental and neuropsychologist whose research and main theory have changed educational thinking since the early 1980s. This chapter provides a historical and contextual background to Gardner's work, and gives a brief outline of Gardner's *multiple intelligences*, identifying the profound influences of this theory upon the early years curriculum and primary practice and exploring how it might be used within practitioner research. Gardner's ideas were instrumental in shaping educational philosophy in the 1980s but are also a vital consideration today. Questions around Gardner's theory will be raised drawing upon significant critiques of his work and we examine how Gardner, in response to criticisms, self-evaluation and other research, reflected and reviewed his ideas over time.

Home background

Howard Gardner was born in 1943 in Scranton, Pennsylvania. His parents had fled Nazi Germany and arrived in the United States in 1938. Howard's older brother died tragically at the age of 7. Howard claims that this and the aspirations that his parents had for Eric were 'transferred to [him] and were important influences on [his] development' (Gardner 2003a). In his autobiographical piece *One Way of Making a Social Scientist*, Gardner (2003a) describes how he 'had been born with crossed eyes, was color blind, myopic, unable to recognize faces, and incapable of binocular vision'. This may have been influential later when Gardner was considering meeting individual needs in the curriculum.

Educational background

Gardner entered Harvard College as an undergraduate in 1961 reading history. However, he found his interests were more towards social sciences rather than history and so changed course to study 'Social Relations', a course which combined psychology, sociology and anthropology. His tutor was Erik Erikson, an influential psychoanalyst whose study explored identity and stages of psychosocial development throughout life from birth to old age. Erikson had previously worked with pioneer psychologists Sigmund and Anna Freud. Erikson's influence led Gardner to veer towards clinical psychology at first, but then Gardner became aware of Jerome Bruner's work as a cognitive psychologist (also working at Harvard) and this, along with Gardner's reading of Jean Piaget's writing, swayed him to pursue cognitive developmental psychology.

Gardner's work and influences

Gardner has been a prolific writer, authoring at least 20 well-regarded books and numerous articles on the human mind, human development, learning, behaviour, the arts and creativity. In 1979, Gardner was able to access a grant which financed his authoring of a book on 'human cognition through discoveries in the biological and behavioural sciences' (Gardner 2003b: 3). The research for this book led to the theory of multiple intelligences. Gardner's *multiple intelligences* derived from his extensive research into specific human abilities, gifts or talents. Gardner decided to call these abilities 'intelligences'; this was a crucial decision and much of the criticism he later faced was due to the choice of the word 'intelligences' rather than 'talents' (Gardner 2003b).

However, his most influential work has been with work on *multiple intelligences* presented in *Frames of Mind: The theory of multiple intelligences* in 1983. This work was first influenced by Gardner's own interest in the arts (he was an enthusiastic pianist and also enjoyed involvement with other arts). When exploring cognitive development psychology he became aware of the lack of interest in the arts and established a quest to 'find a place for the arts within academic psychology' (Gardner 2003b). Further to this, Gardner read the work of Norman Geschwind: neurological research about normal and gifted individuals who suffered brain damage. Gardner was excited by the work of Geschwind and worked with him post-doctorally; Gardner also undertook work on a neuropsychological unit for 20 years, studying 'the organization of human abilities in the brain' (Gardner 2003b).

Gardner's interest in cognitive development had led him to study the work of Jean Piaget and his work on intelligence and the Binet system of measuring a single intelligence (IQ tests). He questioned the need to measure intelligence rather than to explore how intelligence worked (Pound 2005: 64). Gardner considered IQ tests to 'only measure a small part of intelligence; often gave labels to children which would stick such as *bright* or *low ability*; and did not encourage teachers to have high enough expectations of children' (Bruce and Meggitt 2006: 256). He learned that most research on intelligence related to linguistic and logical intelligences and, while he did not deny the existence of a general intelligence, Gardner maintained that human beings could have other areas of strength or talents in particular areas. As a result Gardner initially devised seven types of intelligences:

- *Linguistic* – words and language
- *Logical-Mathematical* – logic and numbers
- *Musical* – music, sound, rhythm
- *Bodily-Kinaesthetic* – body movement control
- *Spatial-Visual* – images and space
- *Interpersonal* – other people's feelings
- *Intrapersonal* – self-awareness.

Later, Gardner was to add a further two types:

- *Naturalist* – natural environment and living things (later in his career Gardner produced empirical evidence for the existence of this new intelligence).
- *Spiritual/Existential* – religion and 'ultimate issues' (Gardner strongly believed that this type of intelligence existed but admitted he did not have sufficient and robust evidence to support it).

Gardner believed that these intelligences were partly genetic but could be nurtured or ignored through a child's culture, social relationships and the environment; he concluded that these intelligences could therefore be developed through education. From his research, Gardner posits that

> All of us have the full range of intelligences: that is what makes us human beings, cognitively speaking; no two individuals have exactly the same intellectual profile, because even with the same genetic make-up (as identical twins), individuals have different experiences; having a strong intelligence does not mean that one necessarily acts intelligently. A person with high mathematical intelligence . . . might waste these abilities in playing the lottery all day or multiplying ten-digit numbers in her head.
>
> (Gardner 2006: 23).

Criticisms of Gardner's multiple intelligence theory

Klein (1997: 337) questions the usefulness of this theory suggesting that the multiple intelligences (MI) are just aspects of the one general intelligence and therefore may only be seen as an 'uninteresting', 'weak' theory. Klein considers the possibility of MI being a 'strong' theory but shows his disappointment in the lack of empirical evidence provided by Gardner to support this. This point is also raised by Sternberg (1999, cited in Kassem et al. 2006: 51): 'although Gardner cites evidence to support his theory he has not carried out research directly to test his model'. Gardner (2003b: 6) and his colleagues developed assessment tools and curriculum activities to diagnose and address individual children's strengths and weaknesses in the various intelligences but Gardner admits that assessment of individual intelligences is 'a difficult task'; critics suggest that it is problematic when trying to isolate and assess a single one of these intelligences rather than a combination of them (Klein 1997).

A key aspect of MI theory is the identification of independent, autonomous intelligences; Gardner's thinking was influenced by brain development research at the time which identified various brain functions being linked to different locations in the brain. However, the notion of intelligences being independent has resulted in critical academic attacks upon Gardner. For example, when looking at different *domains* (broad areas of activity such as disciplines or crafts which have observable levels of competence: Gardner 1993) such as dancing, more than one intelligence is being engaged: the dancer will be drawing upon bodily-kinaesthetic, spatial and musical intelligences. Completing any task involves intelligences working together and thus supports the single general intelligence rather than MI (Klein 1997). In response to this, and based upon Gardner's reviewing the MI theory in the light of new research, Gardner states: 'I have never claimed that intelligences are completely independent; rather, they are relatively independent from one another, as illustrated by the fact that strength in one intelligence does not predict strength or weakness in other intelligences' (Gardner 1998: 99). His later work also shows a move in his thinking about independent intelligences: that intelligences cannot be seen in isolation and need to be considered in the context of a domain; furthermore, he adds, 'Nearly all domains require proficiency in a set of intelligences; and any intelligence can be mobilized for use in a wide array of culturally available domains' (Gardner 1993: xxi).

Gardner cites particular groups of people such as geniuses, child prodigies, and a small number of people with autism and certain disabilities who excel in one domain (savants), as examples of people with a high level of *one* intelligence (Gardner 1983). Klein (1997) contests this, arguing that specific experts in a particular field often are expert in other fields too (for example, the English television celebrity, Jonathan Miller, is accomplished in several fields such as medicine and the performing arts). Klein also questions that savants, while being outstanding in one particular type of task, are not always excellent across that domain: if a person had a high level of bodily-kinaesthetic intelligence should they be excellent in all physical activity? Or, should a high level of linguistic intelligence mean that we can expect that person to excel in reading, writing, verbal expression and processing received language?

In considering conditions such as dyslexia, Gardner offers the suggestion that these students may have a low level of linguistic intelligence, that they are limited in the whole domain of literacy, not just one aspect of it: 'I completely disagree with the claim that dyslexic students typically are normal in aspects of language other than reading' (Gardner 1998: 100). However, Klein (1997: 383) again refutes this by stating that a person suffering from dyslexia may struggle to read but may be equal to their peers in other aspects of literacy such as listening skills.

Another criticism is that the mastery of a task does not totally rely upon whether a person is strong in a particular intelligence but also relies upon *the acquisition of knowledge and development and practice of skills*. The question is raised as to whether having a strength in an intelligence results in the individual excelling in that domain or, whether early stimulation, tuition, emersion, involvement and encouragement promotes curiosity and practice so that the individual becomes a master of that domain and hence will develop a strength in that particular intelligence: which comes first (Klein 1997)?

Furthermore, Barnett et al. (2006: 103) echo a common criticism of Gardner's MI theory: that it is too simplistic and 'obvious'. However, they counter this by adding that many big theories can be seen to be common sense and obvious now, but these, including Gardner's theory, were revolutionary when they were first formulated and published and were very influential in changing the landscape of primary education.

Gardner has responded to these criticisms since the 1990s, particularly in the paper 'Multiple intelligences after twenty years' (Gardner 2003b) and in the book *Howard Gardner Under Fire* (Schaler 2006), and these responses have shown how his MI theory is organic and has developed to accommodate more recent neuroscientific studies and educational research; it is, indeed, still developing and open to future researchers to pursue (Gardner 2003b).

How Gardner's MI theory has influenced early primary and primary education

Howard Gardner was a psychologist and author of six books by the time he had researched and published his theory of MI in *Frames of Mind* in 1983. He expected this book to be well received by psychologists, following the success of his earlier works, but he did not expect such enormous interest from educationalists, who seized upon this with great enthusiasm: 'I was amazed at how many individuals said that they wanted to revise their educational practices in the light of the MI theory' (Gardner 2003b: 6). During the next couple of decades Gardner's MI theory could be seen in the curricula and pedagogy of a multitude of schools around the world. This realization of the value of the theory to education led Gardner to pursue research into the education sector, resulting in his designing curriculum and assessment instruments to measure and document learning (Gardner 2003b).

Gardner had always had a strong interest in the arts and held committed beliefs against a school curriculum which favoured English and mathematics over other subjects. He saw ways in which the MI theory could raise the profile of the arts in the curriculum and he championed the idea of teaching subject content through a variety of ways to suit the prominent intelligence profiles of the pupils; for example, if a child found learning through a traditional teaching method difficult, then the teacher was encouraged to try teaching using a different approach such as teaching history through drama or mathematics through creative arts. Gardner, as a result of his work in schools, promoted the notion of different learning styles which was also being introduced by the research of his contemporaries (Honey and Mumford 1982; Kolb 1985). Although the idea of children having preferred methods of learning was initially suggested as early as the 1920s by educational pioneers such as Montessori, the early 1980s saw the emergence of VAK learning styles (VAK stands for visual, auditory and kinaesthetic: *visual* means learning through seeing, visual aids, demonstration, etc.; *auditory* means learning through sound, listening, verbal instruction, etc.; and *kinaesthetic* means learning through touching, holding, hands-on experience, doing, etc.). Gardner's MI theory supported this approach well.

Drawing upon the MI theory and taking new research in brain development into account, Colin Rose developed the concept of *accelerated learning*, publishing a book with this title in 1985. Accelerated learning swept through primary schools around the globe purporting to enable children to learn more quickly by teaching through methods which addressed a child's preferred learning style and which matched his or her particular profile of intelligences. Gardner's work also inspired research into other types of intelligence such as the emotional intelligence work of Daniel Goleman and moral intelligence studies of Robert Coles since 2000. The MI theory has also had a strong influence upon the principles of early years curricula.

The English early years curriculum – *Curriculum Guidance for the Foundation Stage* (Qualifications and Curriculum Authority (QCA) 2000) and the *Statutory Framework for the Early Years Foundation Stage* (DfES 2007) – reflects the ideas that children have different learning styles and that all areas of learning are of equal importance: 'Children develop and learn in different ways and at different rates and all areas of Learning and Development are equally important and inter-connected' (DCSF 2008c: 9). The government initiative for personalized learning (DCSF 2008b) highlights the need for teachers to acknowledge, assess, identify and address children's individual learning needs, taking into account children's different learning styles and particular strengths and weaknesses. The introduction of intervention programmes to meet individual learning needs (*Every Child a Reader, Every Child a Writer, Every Child Counts*) and the

Assessment for Learning Strategy (DCSF 2008a) have provided schools with a framework for assessing and addressing children's particular learning needs through appropriate teaching methods, activities and resources.

Misinterpretations of Gardner's MI theory by practitioners

The above influences of Gardner's work upon early years curriculum and pedagogy have been irrefutably beneficial in ensuring every child has equal opportunity to maximize their learning. However, as Gardner himself noted, there have been 'a number of misinterpretations of the theory' (2003b: 8) and these misuses of the MI theory can be commonly found among practitioners when they have only a surface understanding of his research. A common misconception is to simplify the MI theory, which can lead to the belief that each child has only one learning style (either visual, or auditory, or kinaesthetic); a deeper study of Gardner would lead to an understanding that all children learn through a mixture of each of these styles, but there is usually a preference towards one or two of them. This suggests that all lessons should include all three approaches to maximize children's learning. Gardner does not believe 'that intelligences are the same as learning styles' or 'that people actually have consistent learning styles' (Woolfolk et al. 2008: 135).

Furthermore, with only a slight grasp of Gardner's work, it is easy for practitioners to force tentative links between a child's achievement and multiple intelligences. For example, if a child appears talented at drawing cartoons it does not necessarily mean that he or she has a high level of spatial-visual intelligence: it could just be that the child has an older sibling who has demonstrated this drawing style and so the child has copied and spent much time practising this one style. Klein (1997) cites a case of a chess master whose expertise might suggest an intelligence profile strong in spatial-visual intelligence (as chess involves movement and visual patterns); however, much cognitive research on the mastery of chess (for example, Ericsson and Smith 1991, cited in Klein 1997: 382) shows that these abilities 'contribute little to its mastery' and 'chess masters are no better than other persons at spatial tasks, except at recognizing strategically significant board arrangements' (Chase and Simon 1973; Pfau and Murphy 1988, both cited in Klein 1997: 382).

How Gardner's MI theory can inform practitioner research

For practitioners to call upon Gardner's multiple intelligence theory effectively to support their research, they need to be fully aware of Gardner's changing beliefs over time and the contribution of new research. Practitioners need to take heed of Gardner's warnings that this theory is to be considered not as physical brain functions but rather a putative concept, initially genetic and then a social construct in which we can identify children's talents and needs in a wide range of domains and offer children more suitable ways, in addition to logical/linguistic, in which they can learn effectively.

Gardner's theory of multiple intelligences can be supportive for the following research topics or sub-areas:

- The importance of creative development, personal, social and emotional development, knowledge and understanding of the world, physical development within the early years curriculum; and the arts, humanities, physical education (PE) and science in the primary curriculum
- Different strategies to teaching curriculum subjects
- The *Every Child Matters* agenda
- Personalized learning, differentiation, individual needs and inclusion
- VAK and learning styles
- Supporting learning of specific groups of children such as gifted and talented, special educational needs (SEN) and English as an alternative language (EAL)
- Children with specific disabilities, such as dyslexia, autism, attention deficit/hyperactivity disorder (ADHD), behavioural difficulties
- Different approaches to early years education, for example Reggio Emilia, Steiner/Waldorf, Montessori
- Cognitive development theory.

Concluding thoughts

Gardner's theory of multiple intelligences rocked the international realms of education. He did not set out to contest the idea of a general intelligence or to affect the educational sector, but he did, by using the term 'intelligences' instead of 'talents', by promoting the idea that children are individuals with different cognitive strengths in different domains and who have different ways of learning, and by highlighting the value of the arts in a curriculum which was overweighted by logical or linguistical importance. His theory was not based on robust empirical evidence and so came 'under fire' (Schaler 2006) but we need to ask, as White (2004, cited in Woolfolk et al. 2008: 137) considers, does it matter if the research is 'flaky' if it leads to good practice and children having 'more self-confidence and the desire to learn'?

Case studies

The following case studies show how Gardner's MI theory can be seen in practice, giving examples of observable characteristics and actions which may suggest a child's strength in a particular intelligence. The case studies can initially be used to further the understanding of intelligences; a deeper consideration of them could stimulate thinking on how a practitioner can use this information to personalize provision.

The data for these case studies have been gathered from four different Foundation Stage settings – reception classes in three different schools and a nursery. They are the results of observing the children over a period of time, talking to members of staff and consulting records.

Case study 3.1: Linguistic intelligence

Kiren is a girl aged 4 years 1 month and currently attends a nursery within a children's centre. The centre is in an economically deprived area, which contains a number of single-parent families and some recently arrived ethnic communities. Kiren is bilingual and lives with both parents.

She learns new words rapidly and has a good vocabulary for her age both in English and in her first language. She often initiates conversations with her key worker and will tell her about events which have happened at home. She also talks to her peers confidently, using simple sentences.

Kiren listens carefully to the adults within the setting and also to her peers. At group time she always listens to the other children's responses and will confidently speak in simple sentences when it is her turn to speak.

She enjoys listening to stories and will often choose to look at books herself. She holds these correctly and runs her finger along the text as she retells the story. She also enjoys rhymes and when a story contained rhyming words she commented upon it saying that 'it sounded the same'.

Kiren often chooses to play where there is an opportunity to write and she handles writing tools with some confidence and a fair degree of control. When she has committed marks to paper she will often explain to an adult what it says demonstrating that she is aware that writing conveys meaning. She can form a number of letters and is able to identify some of their sounds. She successfully writes her first name on a daily basis when she enters the setting.

The above evidence would suggest that Kiren has well-developed linguistic intelligence.

Case study 3.2: Spatial/visual intelligence

David is a boy aged 5 years 3 months and currently attends a reception class in a primary school. The school is in a very economically deprived area, which contains a high number of single-parent families and there are many social issues. David lives with his mother and has no siblings.

He enjoys all art activities, both creating his own artefacts and examining those made by other artists. His drawings particularly of people are very detailed and mature for his age, revealing that he has good observational skills. When painting he chooses his colours carefully and can become upset if the colour is not exactly as he wants it to be. His fine motor control is good and he can handle a number of tools with a good degree of control.

David's hand–eye coordination is well developed for his age. He can throw and catch a ball better than most of his peers. When playing in the sand/water trays he can pour and fill the containers with a good degree of control.

When art activities are not available within the class, David's next favoured option is jigsaws, where he is adept. He completes the reception class jigsaws with great ease and his teacher has had to borrow jigsaws from Key Stage 1 classes to provide a greater challenge.

When using the construction equipment, David builds some imaginative models. He enjoys following the manufacturer's suggestions and can follow a two-dimensional representation of a three-dimensional model with ease.

In maths-focused sessions, David can match two- and three-dimensional shapes well, finds pictograms easy to interpret and understands and uses positional language confidently. He can find objects by following directions. He is adept at playing 'Kim's game' and can always remember which items have been removed from the set and where they were.

When David is not on task, he does not talk to his peers or fidget but prefers to daydream and will sit quietly for a period of time if the staff allow him. This and the above evidence seems to suggest that his spatial/visual intelligence is well developed.

Case study 3.3: Logical/mathematical intelligence

Poppy is a girl aged 4 years 5 months and currently attends the same nursery as Kiren (above). Poppy lives with both parents and has two siblings, one older and one younger.

Every morning when the register is taken, the children are encouraged to count how many are present. Poppy loves to join in this activity and when asked to count on her own will count all the children with one-to-one correspondence up to 13 (the maximum number in the group). She remembers numbers quite easily – for example the key worker asked how many children had been there the day before and she answered with confidence. She has memorized her house number and her seven-digit telephone number.

She will often count objects spontaneously in her play, for example the number of sheep in the farm, the number of birds on the computer screen. In numeracy-focused adult-led activities Poppy excels. For example a recent activity was to split a group of four play people in different ways on a double-decker bus, placing some on the top deck and some below. The key worker asked how many people were on the bus in the different arrangements. Poppy was the only child who consistently was correct, explaining that there were still four. She explained that there were three people on the top deck and one more below was four.

She enjoys pattern work and has produced some simple repeating patterns using a variety of materials, for example printing, peg boards, shapes, computer games. One of her favourite activities is to play on the computer and she will spend a whole free-choice session working her way through all the games on the CD-ROM, returning to the pattern making game at frequent intervals.

The above evidence seems to suggest that Poppy's logical/mathematical intelligence is well developed.

Case study 3.4: Musical intelligence

Ricky is a boy aged 4 years 10 months and currently attends a reception class in a primary school. The school is in the same very economically deprived area as Kiren and Poppy's school. Ricky lives with his mother and has one younger brother.

Ricky likes music sessions – he enjoys singing and learns songs quickly. He is not as articulate as his peers and does not speak very frequently so this ability to learn the words to songs was seen as unusual. He can tap/clap rhythms well, which also surprised his teacher, as he is not as well coordinated as his peers. He enjoys listening to music and often comments on the music he hears in the daily act of worship.

When playing Ricky will often hum to himself and does not realize he is making a sound. If the musical instruments are available he will choose these and will spend most of the session exploring the sounds they make, making up short rhythmic patterns.

He is sensitive to environmental sounds – the school has an outdoor area with a projecting plastic roof. When it rains heavily Ricky goes inside as he does not like the noise. When he first joined the class he would cover his ears and cry. Walking around the local area he still becomes upset if there is too much traffic and thus considerable noise.

The above evidence seems to suggest that Ricky's musical intelligence is well developed.

Case study 3.5: Bodily-kinaesthetic intelligence

Greg is a boy aged 4 years 9 months and currently attends the same nursery as Kiren and Poppy. Greg lives with his mother and has three siblings, two older brothers and one younger sister.

For his age Greg has good gross motor control. He always chooses activities which involve movement, preferably outside, either on the bikes or playing football with two of his peers. He can kick a football in the direction he wants. When he is running he can change direction to avoid obstacles. He negotiates the bikes around the bike area well. He maintains his balance when walking on raised stepping stones, climbs stairs with ease and navigates the climbing frame confidently. He enjoys rolling and crawling up and down the grassed bank. In PE sessions he can move backwards, forwards and sideways. He can jump off equipment and land safely and he can hop using either leg.

Greg can fairly accurately throw and catch a smaller ball, the latter suggesting he has good hand–eye coordination. He is quite adept at making things such as models with building bricks and he made an interesting aeroplane out of wood and nails, using a saw and a hammer. He sometimes enjoys taking models made of construction material apart and reassembling them but his usual choice are activities where he uses his whole body.

In group sessions unless there is a lot of movement he can fidget quite a lot and finds it difficult to sit still. Greg prefers to have songs, stories or rhymes which involve action. His favourite song is 'Heads, Shoulders, Knees and Toes': he finds it easy to indicate all the relevant body parts.

In other aspects of development such as language and personal and social development Greg is performing as expected for his age which suggests that his bodily-kinaesthetic intelligence could be predominant.

Case study 3.6: Interpersonal intelligence

Salma is a girl aged 5 years 9 months and currently attends a reception class in a primary school. The school is in an economically deprived area, which contains a high number of well-established ethnic minority families. Salma lives with both her parents and five other siblings – four older sisters and one younger brother. English is her second language.

She is quite an extrovert child who prefers not to be on her own. She is a popular member of the class and others choose to play with her. When the class are asked to choose a partner she is often one of the first to be picked.

Salma works well as part of a group and can take turns and share fairly. She enjoys helping other children with their work – sometimes too much! She regularly chooses to play in the role play area with a small group of peers. When she is there she often allocates roles to her peers and leads the direction of the play and her peers are happy to accept her leadership.

Whenever a child falls over in the outside area and needs assistance, Salma is often the one who comforts the child and escorts him/her to a member of staff, which indicates she can empathize with her peers. When the class were studying the topic of feelings she demonstrated she could express a range of feelings and also interpret the facial expressions of others, above average for her age.

This evidence would suggest that Salma's interpersonal intelligence is well developed.

Suggested further reading

Gardner, H. (1983) *Frames of Mind: The theory of multiple intelligences*. New York: Basic Books.
Gardner, H. (2006) *Multiple Intelligences: New horizons*. New York: Basic Books.
Schaler, J.A. (ed.) (2006) *Howard Gardner Under Fire: The rebel psychologist faces his critics*. Chicago, IL: Open Court.

References

Barnett, S., Ceci, S. and Williams, W. (2006) 'Is the ability to make a bacon sandwich a mark of intelligence? And other issues: Some reflections on Gardner's theory of multiple intelligences.' In J.A. Schaler (ed.) *Howard Gardner Under Fire: The rebel psychologist faces his critics*. Chicago, IL: Open Court.
Bruce, T. and Meggitt, C. (2006) *Child Care and Education*, 4th edn. Abingdon: Hodder Arnold.
Chase, W.G. and Simon, H.A. (1973) 'The mind's eye in chess.' In W.G. Chase (ed.) *Visual Information Processing*. New York: Academic Press.
DCSF (2008a) *Assessment for Learning Strategy*. DCSF 00341-2008. Nottingham: DCSF.
DCSF (2008b) *Personalised Learning: A Practical Guide*. DCSF 00844-2008. Nottingham: DCSF.
DCSF (2008c) *The Statutory Framework for the Early Years Foundation Stage*. 00261-2008 PCK-EN. Nottingham: DCSF.
Department for Education and Skills (DfES) (2007) *The Early Years Foundation Stage: Setting the standards for learning, development and care for children from birth to five*. Nottingham: DfES.
Ericsson, K.A. and Smith, J. (1991) 'Prospects and limits of the empirical study of expertise: An introduction.' In K.A. Ericsson and J. Smith (eds) *Towards a General Theory of Expertise: Prospects and limits*. Cambridge: Cambridge University Press.
Gardner, H. (1983) *Frames of Mind: The theory of multiple intelligences*. New York: Basic Books.
Gardner, H. (1993) *Frames of Mind: The theory of multiple intelligences*, 2nd edn. London: Fontana.
Gardner, H. (1995) 'Reflections on multiple intelligences: Myths and messages.' *Phi Delta Kappan*, 77(3): 200–208.

Gardner, H. (1998) 'A reply to Perry D. Klein's "Multiplying the Problems of Intelligence by Eight".' *Canadian Journal of Education*, 23(1): 96–102.

Gardner, H. (2003a) *One Way of Making a Social Scientist*. Available at www.howardgardner.com (accessed February 2010).

Gardner, H. (2003b) '*Multiple intelligences after twenty years*.' Paper presented at the American Educational Research Association, Chicago, IL, 21 April.

Gardner, H. (2006) *Multiple Intelligences: New horizons*. New York: Basic Books.

Honey, P. and Mumford, A. (1982) *The Manual of Learning Styles*. Maidenhead: Honey Press.

Kassem, D., Mufti, E. and Robinson, J. (eds) (2006) *Education Studies: Issues and critical perspectives*. Maidenhead: Open University Press.

Klein, P.D. (1997) 'Multiplying the problems of intelligence by eight: A critique of Gardner's theory'. *Canadian Journal of Education*, 22(4): 377–394.

Kolb, D. (1985) *Learning Style Inventory*. Boston, MA: McBer.

Pfau, H.D. and Murphy, M.D. (1998) 'Role of verbal knowledge in chess skill.' *American Journal of Psychology*, 101: 73–86.

Pound, L. (2005) *How Children Learn*. Leamington Spa: Step Forward.

Qualifications and Curriculum Authority (QCA) (2000) *Curriculum Guidance for the Foundation Stage*. London: QCA.

Rose, C. (1985) *Accelerated Learning*. New York: Dell.

Schaler, J.A. (ed.) (2006) *Howard Gardner Under Fire: The rebel psychologist faces his critics*. Chicago, IL: Open Court.

Sternberg, R.J. (1999) 'Intelligence.' In R.A. Wilson and F.C. Keil (eds) *The MIT Encyclopedia of the Cognitive Sciences*. Cambridge, MA: MIT Press.

White, J. (2004) 'Howard Gardner: The myth of multiple intelligences.' Lecture at Institute of Education, University of London, 17 November. Available at http://k1.ioe.ac.uk.school/mst/LTU/phil/HowardGardner_171104.pdf (accessed 12 November 2009).

Woolfolk, A., Hughes, M. and Walkup, V. (2008) *Psychology in Education*. Harlow: Pearson Education.

4 Using activity theory to examine the factors shaping the learning partnerships in a parent and child 'stay and play' session

Martin Needham

Introduction: an overview of the purpose of the research

This chapter reflects on the application of the concept of 'activity', developed by Vygotsky in the 1930s, which I have used to support my own doctoral research. The idea of activity is also used by several influential early childhood researchers in order to draw attention to the importance of context in shaping the different roles, rules and purposes that participants hold in shared activities (Rogoff 1990; Hedegaard and Fleer 2008). My own study seeks to explore interactions between practitioners, parents/carers and children in the context of parent and toddler groups. I am interested in the ways that family sociocultural factors may harmonize or clash with educational cultures (Rogoff 1998; Brooker 2002). In this chapter I use examples from case studies to show how focusing on activity rather than individuals may throw new light on joint activities or interaction and also creates some interesting methodological discussion.

Cultural historical activity theory (Wells and Claxton 2002), or activity theory for short, has evolved from psychological perspectives but shares some of the features of sociological study in that it examines human behaviour in context rather than in laboratory or test conditions (Hedegaard and Fleer 2008). My personal interest is in the context of parents and children participating jointly in play settings supervised by educational professionals. I find that this offers an opportunity to explore how home and school learning styles complement or clash with each other, exposing the complexity of interactions that are usually taken for granted.

It would seem to be common sense that parent–child interactions may impact upon the child's attitudes to organized educational activities.

Nevertheless the evidence provided by research such as the Effective Provision of Preschool Education (EPPE) study (Sammons et al. 2007) show the child's early home learning environment to be one of the most significant predictors of later educational achievement. The significance of supporting a positive start for children has increasingly been accepted by society and is demonstrated by the increasing level of interest in parenting classes, the number of TV programmes on dealing with difficult children and the broad political commitment to supporting families through Sure Start children's centres (DfES 2007a). However, the nature and flexibility of the learning partnerships between parent and child in this age range is under-researched, particularly in situ, as compared to more controlled experimental conditions. Investigation of the relationship between early years practitioners and parents in support of the child's learning trajectory, in the context of carer and child sessions, may help to refine the approaches employed by, the training for and the funding of such groups. What is 'special' about this particular transition from home to organized group is the extended joint involvement of both parent and child. Such joint involvement offers an insight into some aspects of the interactions the child experiences in the home and potentially some clues about how the child will react to new learning contexts. My research therefore seeks to capture for analysis the triadic relationship between parent, practitioner and child and the possible consequences of this in shaping the child's attitudes towards learning.

I chose to use activity theory as the framework for reflecting on the context of the 'toddler groups' as a unit of analysis because it seemed to offer a different and relevant perspective from which to record and analyse the interactions that were taking place in the groups. The reasons for this choice will be discussed in the next section of this chapter. Three case study examples of child–parent orientations to activities within the setting of parent and toddler groups are reflected upon to illustrate how Yrjö Engeström's model of activity theory is helpful in this context (Engeström et al. 1999; Engeström 2007).

Why does interaction matter?

Many sociocultural researchers are concerned with the type of learning that is promoted in educational contexts. They argue that too much emphasis is placed on the individual as the focus of learning. Mercer (2000) and Rogoff (1990, 1998), for example, interpret Vygotsky's work on the idea of the zone of proximal development (ZPD: see Chapter 1) to mean not only that adults should provide materials and ideas to learners, but also that learners benefit from a dialogue, exchange of ideas or shared thinking with others about how to interpret and perform the activity that is being studied. These researchers argue that the nature of the dialogue taking place within a particular situation plays a role in shaping thinking and attitudes to learning that is often over-looked (Rogoff 1990; Mercer 2000).

Studies of children's learning from early infancy onwards draw attention to the nature of the interactions between adults and children as a key indicator of effective learning. Rogoff (2003) draws attention to a number of studies involving different age groups, but from as young as 7 months old, to illustrate the concept of contingent scaffolding. Contingent scaffolding is adult support that is matched to the level of the child and faded out as the child assumes greater control of what is to be learned. She notes how this mode of interaction appears to be a more common phenomenon among middle-class European and American mothers (Rogoff 1998). The concept of scaffolding was developed by Wood and Bruner (Wood et al. 1976; Wood 1998) suggests that children developed more consistent abilities to resolve problems where the adult allowed the child to retain as much control of the process as possible and drew the child's attention to significant aspects of the process. Jordan (2004), studying preschool teachers involved in interactions, describes an additional distinction in adult–child interactions extending the analysis of scaffolding. She points to improved understanding arising through 'co-construction' where, as with the existing description scaffolding, the adult is building upon the child's lead but in addition the interaction with children features the following:

- Co-constructing meaning, including hearing children and getting to know what they think;
- Questioning techniques with no particular knowledge out in the teacher's head, aware of their interests, not interrupting them, allowing silences, following children's leads;
- Making links in thinking across time and activities through visiting children's ideas and interests, making links between sources of ideas, knowing children really well;
- Developing full, two way inter-subjectivity with children, through sharing their own ideas with children to extend their current interests, often as an in depth project, entering the child's fantasy play, valuing and giving voice to children's activities, respectfully checking that a child would like the offered assistance.
  (Jordan 2004: 40–41)

In a detailed study of interactions in preschools as part of the EPPE project Sylva (Sylva et al. 2004) showed that more frequent employment of co-constructive, sustained shared thinking in practitioner–child interactions were associated with enhanced longer term educational achievement.

My own research investigates the modes of interaction employed in parent and toddler groups which give children the opportunity to participate in learning in a preschool-like setting for the first time. I wanted to find out how parent and toddler groups encouraged children to learn with others, the extent to which shared thinking was employed, and whether the activities and interactions offered by the adults helped the children to participate in scaffolding and co-constructive exchanges.

Why choose activity theory?

In the opening section of this chapter I identified my interest, not only in how an individual learns in isolation, but also in how the individual learns in the process of doing things with others. With this as a starting point, cultural historical activity quickly began to attract my attention because it sets out to explore exactly these sorts of situations and because it is based in the ideas of Lev Vygotsky. Vygotsky's ideas about learning are increasingly influential in the pedagogical practice of early education particularly and feature in many key textbooks (Bruce and Meggit 2002) as well as the Early Years Foundation Stage (QCA 2000; DfES 2007b).

The view of knowledge as 'socially framed' was set out philosophically by Marx (Marx and Engels 1976) and then developed in a psychological framework by Vygotsky (1978), Leont'ev (1978) and others (Wertsch 1998; Engeström et al. 1999; Daniels 2001). Knowledge, it is argued, is not something that exists preformed to be discovered, it is rather developed through the evolution of human activity. Humanity has developed both physical tools and mental tools through experience and the desire to achieve certain goals. Knowledge will always be evolving in the light of what we seek to do and will always build upon the cultural practices of the past. We develop through learning to participate in the use of the physical tools (writing materials) and mental tools (i.e. language) that are available to us to adapt to the environment in which we find ourselves. Theories of activity set out a range of approaches that seek to look, not at the learner alone, but at the learner as part of a system of mutually affective elements involving the way people use tools in a particular place.

Conceptual tools

The set of approaches referred to as activity theory (Engeström et al. 1999), cultural historical activity theory (Wells and Claxton 2002) and sociocultural-historical theory (Rogoff 2003; Hedegaard and Fleer 2008) share a focus on subject (actor), object (purpose) and mediating objects (tools). Engeström's description of activity theory sets out what he refers to as a model of third generation of activity theory which also includes rules, community and the division of labour as elements for consideration. This additional layer is added in recognition that subject, mediator and artefact do not operate in isolation in the moment of action, but are influenced by wider cultural factors that shape the context and rules of social engagement.

My own research considers the transition of the child from the more private sphere of 'home, family and friends' into a more public and educational context. It examines how practitioners, parents and child direct learning in the parents and toddlers group context. The approach seeks to identify elements of shared culture and cultural dissonances in relation to supporting learning. In order to capture this exchange I have drawn on models of discourse analysis emerging from activity theory.

Engeström and Middleton (1996) use triangular diagrammatic models to show how individual subjects, their purposes and community are interconnected by the rules for using different culturally developed tools. (Daniels 2008). Engeström's model has been adopted as a template to set out the diagram in Figure 4.1 (Needham 2010) in order to illustrate how these aspects of a particular parent and child session might be recorded.

For the activities analysed in my study, there are often three actors' perspectives that could be considered: parent, child and practitioner depending on the focus of the analysis. Activity is helpful because it highlights that different individual's purposes and interpretation of the materials available in any

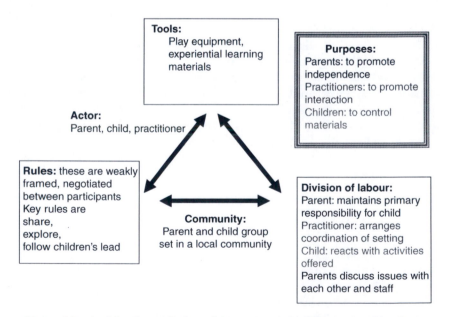

Figure 4.1   Applying Engeström's model to parent and toddler groups. (Needham 2010, adapted from Engeström and Middleton 1996)

activity may be different. Each of the participants brings a different understanding that can potentially help the others to learn to adapt to the activity in new ways, particularly where there are tensions around the purpose of the activity.

It is essential that the researcher sets limits about which aspects of interaction their research will focus upon and who the focus of their study is upon. Rogoff (2003) is a great help in setting out different possibilities for focusing data collection and analysis. In order to generate manageable data Rogoff (2003) suggests that different lenses need to be adopted, such as interpersonal relationships, cultural institutional practices, cultural historical artefacts materials (Pramling-Samuelsson and Fleer 2009). For the purpose of this chapter I am focusing on the purposes of the different stakeholders, parents, children and practitioners, to illustrate how the differences in these purposes might compromise joint activity in the parent and toddler groups studied.

The potential of such an approach is illustrated in research by Pentti Hakkarainen (1999), who examined play in an early years centre using videos of play interactions. Hakkarainen (1999) illustrated how, although the tools and rules might be similar in an early education context, the purposes or 'object' of children's play could be varied. He identified four competing purposes. He suggested that the adults pursued the development of the children both educationally and emotionally. The children pursued satisfaction through both mastery of both social relationships and material content. He was sceptical of the idea that the purpose of play is to resolve conflicts in the child's mind and instead asserted that play from the children's perspective is related to the mastery of tools, with play affording a forum to repeat and try out alternate performances in a relatively low risk and pleasurable physical and social context. He argued that the practitioners' perspective was to pursue more specific skill development in particular individuals rather than contributing to the play in the here and now. The consequence of this conflict of interests he argued might interfere with co-construction of the meaning and action and might cause children to see adults as outsiders and disrupters of their play. Hakkarainen's examples of dialogue illustrate this clash of purposes beautifully as in the following attempt to establish a role play of 'sleeping beauty':

Teacher:	what happened then? Anna was the fairy.
Anna:	No, I want to be the princess.
Teacher:	and Retta was? What happened next? The story goes on
Anna:	we only sit here. Who was the king? You could be the queen and you will be a fairy and I will be the princess. We only sit here (stands up) We all stand here like soldiers. You should do something.
Reeta:	What then?
Anna:	Play the story of course.

Reeta:	of course but how?
Anna:	have you ever heard the tale of sleeping beauty?
Reeta:	Yes
Anna:	then start now
Reeta:	you start
Teacher:	what happens next?

(Hakkarainen 1999: 241)

The girls resist the teacher's efforts to plan a story line in advance, preferring to establish the characters of baby, queen, fairy godmother and evil godmother. In this context the teacher's purposes are satisfied by the negotiation between the girls in terms of developing literacy skills and her participation is minimal. The teacher does not move to participate in the role play; it is the girls who are the players seeking to sustain play that is rich and satisfies their social purpose instead.

Purposes or objects matter because they frame the role adopted by the participants and the nature of the interaction that occurs. It could be argued that when adults seek to enter play in keeping with the children's purpose the interaction could become a more level shared endeavour. Such a move to alter purpose could lead to an amended role and rules of engagement that would need to be adopted by both adults and children but might in more sustained shared thinking.

Data collection methods

Having identified sociocultural activity as a theoretical framework for my own research, it is now appropriate to set out more methodological detail with regard to data collection.

Rogoff (1998, 2003), Hedegaard and Fleer (2008) and Pramling-Samuelson and Fleer (2009) seek to develop ways of using the concept of sociocultural-historical activity to study children in context. In the study of activity, they all suggest, it is not so much that data collection methods have to be of a certain type, but that they should help to answer questions about *how* people are participating in activities. These authors frequently refer to ethnography, a field of sociological and anthropological science which has developed procedures for observing and interviewing people as they live their lives in communities. Fetterman (1989) describes ethnography as the art and science of describing a group or culture. Ethnography affords the researcher the opportunity to record the attitudes and dispositions of those involved in a specific context, taking time to try to view social life from their perspectives and to check their interpretation of what takes place focusing on daily routines to identify patterns of behaviours (Fetterman 1989). Fetterman continues:

the ethnographer enters the field with an open mind, not an empty head, before asking questions in the field, the ethnographer begins with a problem, a theory or model, a research design, specific data collection techniques specific data collection techniques, tools for analysis and a specific writing style.

(Fetterman 1989: 1)

Engeström reviews a range of research work that seeks to apply activity theory to the investigation of working practices in different contexts (Engeström and Middleton 1996). He characterizes these works as 'strips of discourse' embedded in thick ethnographic descriptions of the institutional setting and flow of work actions (Engeström and Middleton 1996: 4). Engeström also draws attention to the value of highlighting the 'multi-voicedness of work practices' (Engeström and Middleton 1996: 5). This is the broad methodological approach that is adopted in the analysis of the case studies in my own research.

In reporting on my own research in this chapter, I seek to describe the exchange of information on supporting children's learning between two possibly different cultures – parents and early years practitioners. Ethnography was deemed to be an appropriate approach for my own research since it seeks participants' perceptions of context in order to mediate observations of their behaviours, in this case to identify their implicit and explicit views of learning and epistemology. The prime tools used in my own research were observation and informal participant interviews that allow for a naturalistic conversation to develop around the participants' perceptions of the context and their role in it. Observations of the children's actions were recorded in a narrative form and illustrative photographs incorporated into accounts in order to provide accessible accounts to form the basis of discussions with parents. Observations and photographs already formed part of the culture of the setting; although they were sometimes a distraction, they were not too intrusive. Parents responded very positively to the accounts produced and were very willing to share their perspectives on activity in their settings.

Context of the case studies

The two parent and toddler groups studied were held under the aegis of separate Sure Start children's centres targeting a disadvantaged area in two different local authorities in the English West Midlands. The sessions were attended by up to ten carers, all parents of either one or two of the children attending. Sessions took place in a converted shop specially adapted into a play space. The children attending were aged between 12 and 36 months; however, several had siblings less than one year of age with them. The sessions were facilitated by two qualified practitioners who set out activities following discussion with parents about children's interests at the end of the previous session. The sessions are often called 'stay and play' and are promoted as opportunities to play with children rather than as a purely social occasion. The sessions are non-directive; the only group activity is a snack and a rhyme time towards the end of the 75-minute session.

Children's purposes

In the first case study, Lucy's purpose appears to be to collect and file away different objects into various containers and it is interesting to see how she responds when her mother tries to introduce a counting element into the play.

Case study 4.1: Lucy

Lucy returns to the chalkboard and stands next to Fazal wiping the board from side to side with a wooden board duster. She picks up the bucket from the stand and moves away. Lucy takes the bucket to the middle of the carpet area where there are corks and tamarind seeds in metal bowls. 'Shall we put the corks into the bucket?' asks her mum and they begin to fill the bucket with corks one by one. 'Shall we count them?' asks her mum. '1 . . . 2 . . . 3' '1 . . . 2 . . . 3'. Lucy moves the bucket a couple of feet away from her mum and puts the corks in handfuls into the bucket. 'Bye,' she waves to her mum and moves to the home corner and watches Joe, who has a bucket and a wooden spoon. She picks up an extra bucket and takes both buckets back to the drawing table. She puts the lids on the felt tip pens. She picks up a rolling pin that has been left on the table, and puts this back with the dough. She gives a drinking glass that has been left on the dough table to Martin, implying it was in the wrong place. She takes a piece of dough and then spends several minutes dividing the dough into small similarly sized pieces on the drawing table.

The mother, in seeking to engage with her daughter's play, chooses to guide her towards a particular numeracy objective, whereas Lucy seems to demonstrate very clearly that this is not what she wishes to do by turning her back on her mother. Lucy's mother seeks to direct Lucy's learning by modelling counting the objects with an invitation to Lucy to join. The mother's offered scaffold begins from her observation of what Lucy is doing, but Lucy seems far more orientated to categorizing and sorting objects, which is a precursor to counting and cardinality. In many of the episodes observed in the study children seemed to be motivated to seek to control the objects available to them. This episode resembles the example of interaction from Hakkarainen's (1999) account in that the participants' purposes are not complementary to each other.

Parents' purposes

In the second case study, the mother's purposes are perhaps still not completely harmonized with the child's, but are accepted and engaged with by the child. Ahmed has been happily fishing objects out of the pan of water and then dropping them back in, content with retrieving the objects from under the water and releasing them and watching them fall back into the water. His mother also adopts a directive teaching role guiding the episode towards recognisable curriculum objective around shape names. In this particular episode, by contrast to the episode with Lucy, Ahmed is happy to participate in the reciprocal role of pupil to his mother as teacher. The opportunity to demonstrate his skills in the area of identifying the shapes offers very positive feedback for Ahmed. In both these first two examples the mother's purposes are geared to towards developing aspects of mathematical language and its application. These illustrate a sense of scaffolding used by Jordan (2004) where the adult has a clear objective in mind and seeks to support the child's learning towards this. In this second example the mother has created a simple game which employs the type of questioning exchanges that children are likely to encounter in educational settings. Any scaffolding works not so much upon the shape names, which Ahmed already knows, but around the behaviours expected in the educational environment.

Case study 4.2: Ahmed

'Missed' she says as the object that Ahmed is dropping back into the pan misses and lands on the floor. He picks up the cup and gives it a tentative lick

'Ne ne [no no]' says mum. Ahmed cannot now reach the objects in the bottom of the pan and Martin helps her to move the pan to a chair so Ahmed can see inside. Another child has started playing on a piano and Ahmed pauses to look for where the sound is coming from. Mum holds a blue cup and Ahmed takes objects from the pan and places into the blue cup.

'Ahmed Star chaieya [I need a], star'

'Star,' says Ahmed handing his mother the star.

'Good boy,' she says enthusiastically and smiling.

There are several shapes in a red bowl that mum offers to Ahmed and she asks him to picks objects from the bowl which she guides 'square dadoh' [pass the square], hexagon dad oh, cup dah doh [give me the cup], Ys me dadoh [give me this thing] as Ahmed passes the objects from the bowl and drops them into the pan. Again, when she says 'star dado' [give me the star], Ahmed selects the appropriate shape and she smiles and says 'Good boy'. 'Missed' she says as the objects that Ahmed is dropping back into the pan misses and lands on the floor he picks up the cup and gives it a tentative lick.

'Ne ne [no no],' says mum.

These case studies illustrate that support offered by the adult can vary in success depending on how well it marries with the child's interests and readiness to engage with the adult's scaffold. It is important to point out that these are only illustrative examples and not necessarily typical of parent's purposes in the group.

Practitioners' purposes

In the third case study, the practitioner responds closely to the interest that Abas appears to demonstrate in the activity. He is clearly engrossed by the glitter falling from his hand back to the table top. The adult extension offered conforms much more to his intentions. This is more illustrative of Jordan's description of co-construction where adult and child exchange ideas about the materials they are engaging with.

The practitioner joins in with Abas's activity rather than generating a new activity: she introduces a new way to move the glitter from the hand and sustains the activity suggesting by her actions a genuine level of approval and appreciation.

Case study 4.3: Abas

Abas moves from the home corner area to stand at the large tray of gold glitter where Julie is already sitting talking with Jane. Mum remains behind watching from the other side of the room. Abas picks up handfuls of the gold glitter from the tray and holds them up.

'Are you squeezing them?' asks Julie. He allows the glitter to fall out of his hand. He looks up at two parents standing nearby and watches them talking as he feels the glitter in the tray with his fingers. He presses both palms into the glitter and studies each one before clapping his hands together hard and watching the glitter sprays off in both directions. He repeats this touching then clapping several times. He sprinkles the glitter from one hand onto the other.

'Are you sprinkling it from hand to hand?' asks Julie.

Abas suddenly looks towards his mother. 'Mummy,' he calls.

'I'm just here' she reassures him from the home corner area. He goes over to her and brings her back to the glitter tray and he resumes pouring the glitter.

'Sparkles,' says Julie. Abas repeats the touching and clapping.

'This is why we come here so we don't have this mess at home,' says mum.

Abas shows a palm full of glitter to Julie who says 'ready' as she indicates that she is going to blow the glitter. They blow together, Abas laughs out loud and the others also laugh. They repeat this.

Jane, who had left sometime before, returns to the glitter tray and Abas moves off towards the washroom with his mum. They return shortly and mum again remains on the other side of the room while Abas returns to the glitter to continue blowing the glitter gently from his hands. Jane has placed a large baby doll in the tray and Abas sprinkles glitter onto its forehead. He blows a palm full of glitter over the doll.

'That was a great big puff of wind,' says Julie, as Abas looks to her and laughs out loud again. He heads back over to his mum and draws her with him towards the bathroom.

'He just likes to use the hand-dryer,' she explains, 'that is all it is.'

Abas soon returns to the glitter tray. He holds the baby by the waist and dips its feet gently in the glitter. He puts the doll down and holds another handful of glitter towards Julie. 'Do you want to put it on my hand?'

He sprinkles the glitter onto Julie's hand.

'Oh wow!' she says.

Abas tentatively licks the glitter. 'It doesn't taste nice,' says Julie.

Abas tries to head for the washroom a third time and mum catches him by the waist and turns him round saying that he doesn't need to wash his hands until he is finished. He returns to the glitter tray and he holds up another handful of glitter for Julie to blow, which she does. Abas then moves towards the washroom again where he uses the hand-dryer to blow the glitter of his hands. He then washes his hands and then blows them dry supported by his mother. He then skips back from the bathroom to the glitter tray.

Implications for supporting interaction in parent and toddler groups

Studying the parents' purposes through interviews as well as observation revealed occasions where they appeared to be in opposition to children's and practitioners'. In addition to some parents sometimes pursuing some traditional educational curricula objectives, many parents sought to support their children in developing independence from themselves. This was often manifest in parents allowing children to investigate materials for themselves with little adult interaction. This was at times counter to the practitioners' purpose of promoting interaction between parent and child. I do not wish to imply this is a negative. Whalley and the Pen Green Team (2007) have noted discomfort with adults being overly directive and clearly framed rules around allowing space for children's purposes to become apparent in more open ended interactive exchanges, however, many of the more directive engagements seemed to engage and extend children's activities.

In relation to roles, a workable compromise between competing perspectives on the role of the adult in supporting learning, seemed to be for the parents to be close by and supportive, thus giving the children attention but at the same time giving the children space to explore independently. There is a potential here for interaction to be reduced when I would argue that children might find it helpful to experience a balance between independent and collaborative learning (Rogoff 1998). My extended research suggests that more collaborative interactions might require more careful explanation, planning and modelling if the group leaders are to achieve this if it is one of their stated objectives.

Reflections the insights offered by 'activity'

This chapter has set out some of the basic principles of approaches to research employing the concept of sociocultural-historical activity. The 'purposes, rules and roles' framework offers a helpful reminder of the type of data that it is important to collect in order to develop a fuller picture of what different actors believe is taking place in a social context. If the researcher has the time capacity for deeper investigation, these areas are also rich in possibility for exploring motivation in a social context. What are the unwritten rules? What are the tacit agreements between people that allow the activity to take place? Thus the researcher can use activity theory to develop a deeper, richer picture of a given social context. Engeström et al. (1999) argue that as a more detailed understanding of context develops, so the points of tension between participants become clearer. As points of tension are revealed and discussed so then can opportunities for change can be explored.

Suggested further reading

Daniels, H. (2008) *Vygotsky and Research*. Abingdon: Routledge.
Hedegaard, M. and Fleer, M. (2008) *Studying Children: A cultural historical approach*. Maidenhead: Open University Press.
Rogoff, B. (1990) *Apprenticeship in Thinking: Cognitive development in social context*. New York: Oxford University Press.

References

Brooker, L. (2002) *Starting School: Young children learning cultures*. Buckingham: Open University Press.
Bruce, T. and Meggit, C. (2002) *Childcare and Education*. London: Hodder & Stoughton.
Daniels, H. (2001) *Vygotsky and Pedagogy*. London: RoutledgeFalmer.
Daniels, H. (2008) *Vygotsky and Research*. Abingdon: Routledge.
DfES (2007a) *The Children's Plan: Building brighter futures*. Nottingham: DfES.

DfES (2007b) *The Early Years Foundation Stage: Setting the standards for learning, development and care for children from birth to five.* Nottingham: DfES.

Engeström, Y. (2007) 'Putting Vygotsky to work.' In H. Daniels, M. Cole and J.V. Wertsch (eds) *The Cambridge Companion to Vygotsky.* New York: Cambridge University Press.

Engeström, Y. and Middleton, D. (1996) *Cognition and Communication at Work.* New York: Cambridge University Press.

Engeström, Y., Miettinen, R. and Punamaki, R.J. (eds) (1999) *Perspectives on Activity Theory.* Cambridge: Cambridge University Press.

Fetterman, D.M. (1989) *Ethnography: Step by step.* London: Sage.

Hakkarainen, P. (1999) 'Play and motivation.' In Y. Engeström, R. Miettinen and R.J. Punamaki (eds) *Perspectives on Activity Theory.* Cambridge: Cambridge University Press.

Hedegaard, M. and Fleer, M. (2008) *Studying Children: A cultural historical approach.* Maidenhead: Open University Press.

Jordan B. (2004) 'Scaffolding learning and co-constructing understandings.' In A. Anning, J. Cullen and M. Fleer (eds) *Early Childhood Education.* London: Sage.

Leont'ev, A.N. (1978) *Activity, Consciousness, and Personality.* Englewood Cliffs, NJ: Prentice-Hall.

Marx, K. and Engels, F. (1976) *Critique of Modern German Philosophy According to its Representatives Fuerbach, Bauer and Stirner.* In *Karl Marx and Frederick Engels Collected Works,* Volume 5. Moscow: Progress.

Mercer, N. (2000) *Words and Minds.* London: Routledge.

Needham, M. (2010) *'Learning to Learn in Supported Parent and Toddler Groups: A sociocultural investigation.'* London: Institute of Education, University of London.

Pramling-Samuelsson, I. and Fleer, M. (2009) *Play and Learning in Early Childhood Settings.* Dordrecht: Springer.

Qualifications and Curriculum Authority (QCA) (2000) *Guidance for the Foundation Stage.* London: QCA.

Rogoff, B. (1990) *Apprenticeship in Thinking: Cognitive development in social context.* New York: Oxford University Press.

Rogoff, B. (1998) 'Cognition as a collaborative process.' In D. Kuhn and R.S. Siegler (eds) *Handbook of Child Psychology.* New York: Wiley.

Rogoff, B. (2003) *The Cultural Nature of Human Development.* Oxford: Oxford University Press.

Sammons, P., Sylva, K., Melhuish, E., Siraj-Blatchford, I., Taggart, B., Grabbe, Y. and Bareau, S. (2007) *Influences on Children's Attainment and Progress in Key Stage 2: Cognitive outcomes in Year 5.* London: Institute of Education, University of London.

Sylva, K., Sammons, P., Siraj-Blatchford, I. and Taggart, B. (2004) *The Final Report: Effective pre-school education.* London: Institute of Education, University of London.

Vygotsky, L.S. (1978) *Mind in Society*. Cambridge, MA: Harvard University Press.

Wells, G. and Claxton, G. (2002) *Learning for Life in the 21st Century*. London: Blackwell.

Wertsch, J.V. (1998) *Mind as Action*. New York: Oxford University Press.

Whalley, M. and the Pen Green Team (2007) *Involving Parents in their Children's Learning*, 2nd edn. London: Paul Chapman.

Wood, D. (1998) *How Children Think and Learn*. Oxford: Blackwell.

Wood, D., Bruner, J.C. and Ross, G. (1976) 'The role of tutoring in problem solving.' *Journal of Child Psychology and Psychiatry*, 17: 89–100.

5 Developing communities of practice: placing professional individual identity in group interactions

Jenny Worsley

Introduction

The powerful ideas situated in Lave and Wenger's (1991) communities of practice provide a useful framework of how interactions can be analysed and how individual professional identity can be constructed, then facilitated by participation in a community of practice. My interest in Lave and Wenger's ideas originated from my previous research in a children's centre to explore practitioners' perspectives of multidisciplinary working (Worsley 2007). Within this inquiry I offered a tentative model of how multiagency working could be achieved by utilizing Lave and Wenger's ideas around communities of practice and situated learning. In the context of a children's centre this involved the development of 'joint aims', 'a common language', 'collaboration' and 'information sharing'. This led to the adoption of Lave and Wenger's concepts in further research of mature, part-time, early years students studying in higher education and the development of an online community of practice. At the heart of this research was the aim to develop a supportive learning community with a view to continuous improvement of the course that empowered students to achieve. At the same time this research aimed to formalize and make more tacit the processes that may affect the student's personal constructs of their identity during the course.

This chapter identifies the origins and ideas captured by Lave and Wenger (1991) in that individuals inevitably participate in communities and through the use of interaction begin to construct knowledge of the social and cultural practices of any given community. This implies a collective understanding of the community's core cultural values. It also involves the transfer of the knowledge and skills of the more experienced community members to support newly joined or less experienced members using informal or 'situated' learning; thus constructing individual professional identify as well as a community identity. The origin of this theory links to the Vygotskian suggestion that learning is not just an individual solitary process but is socially constructed through shared activity (Daniels 2001). This is further emphasized by Bruner (1999: 150) suggesting that 'learning and thinking are always situated in a cultural setting'. Therefore it is by interacting and negotiating meanings with others that individuals discover what the culture, or in this case the community, is about.

Based on personal postgraduate research in a higher education institution with early years practitioners studying on a foundation degree, I illustrate how the key ideas identified in this chapter can contribute to practice when working and learning with other professionals. Nurturing a community of practice can also offer a model for constructing interactions of professionals from a range of agencies involved in integrated services and in higher education.

Professional individual identity

In recent years there has been a plethora of policy initiatives that have changed the landscape of early year's provision; in particular the Children's Workforce strategy (DfES 2005) recognizes that a highly qualified early years workforce leads to improved quality provision for young children and their families. However, with an increased emphasis on 'joined up' thinking in terms of children's services, there is a requirement for early years practitioners to work collaboratively with other agencies, such as health and social family support and parents. Thus there is an increased emphasis on developing practitioners who have the confidence and skills to achieve these new ways of working, and more importantly, the willingness to continually question their own professionalism and values (Anning and Edwards 2006).

The development of foundation degrees in early years and related areas (DfES 2003) is embedded in inclusive lifelong learning and widening participation policy but has also been linked to the apparent need to up-skill the children's workforce. Various studies have identified how an individual's self-identity, both on a personal and professional level, is influenced by higher level study. Research by Dunne et al. (2008) into the perceived benefits of undertaking a foundation degree by teaching assistants identified the interrelationship between changes in both personal and professional identity. As Dunne et al. (2008: 54) argue, 'the two intersect and lives are not compartmentalised into the professional and the personal self, but events that occur in one area potentially impact upon, and have implications for, other areas'. Penketh and Goddard (2008) also highlighted the integrated nature of mature students' experiences of a foundation degree. It was difficult for these students to separate the academic experience from the social or personal aspects or their work contexts. When entering higher education, students are exposed to a new community of practice with particular sets of traditions, activities and boundaries; however, their participation is also influenced by other aspects of their lives, such as their workplace experiences in terms of their status and how their value as a professional is perceived by their colleagues.

The ideas of Lave and Wenger (1991) in terms of situated learning and communities of practice are useful to consider in this context. They suggest that learning and identity are contextualized in communities of which an individual may belong to. Within these communities an individual develops knowledge of practices prevalent in the community, including norms and values. Wenger (1998) frames issues of identity as a pivot between the social world and the individual:

> Talking about identity in social terms is not denying individuality but viewing the very definition of individuality as something that is part of the practices of specific communities. It is therefore a mistaken dichotomy to wonder whether the unit of analysis of identity should be the community or the person. The focus must be on the process of their mutual constitution.
>
> (Wenger 1998: 146)

This asserts that a person's sense of identity is tied to social reality, thus in this approach, identity formation is seen as a complex and situated phenomenon. For Wenger (2000: 239) 'an identity is not an abstract idea or label, such as a title, an ethnic category, or a personality trait. It is a lived experience of belonging'. To fully capture these ideas of how identity formation is linked to social reality I will explore the key concepts outlined in Lave and Wenger's theory.

Communities of practice

Lave and Wenger (2002) provide a useful framework for analysis of social learning in their theory around communities of practice. For Wenger (1998: 3) current views about learning 'are largely based on the assumption that learning is an individual process, that it has a beginning and an end, that it is best separated from the rest of our activities.' However, Lave and Wenger in their model of 'communities of practice' are suggesting that learning is social in nature and is generated from our experiences of participating in daily life. Therefore learning is not in individual minds as an abstract concept, it is constructed through participation in social practices.

According to Lave and Wenger (1991) we all belong to differing communities of practice, for example, at home, at work, and we connect to several at any given period of time and these often change over the course of our lives. This refers to the notion of a 'nexus of multi-membership' whereby 'we define who we are by the ways we reconcile our various forms of member-ship into one identity' (Wenger 1998: 149). Thus learning takes place through participation and engagement in different activities and through interactions with others, it through these constant interactions that learning reproduces and changes the social structure, or community, in which it takes place. As Wenger (1998) argues:

> learning is an integral part of our everyday lives. It is part of our participation in our communities and organizations. The problem is not that we do not know this, but rather we do not have systematic ways of talking about this familiar experience.
>
> (Wenger 1998: 8)

The point is also made that informal learning is often not acknowledged as learning, particularly within the workplace. It is often regarded as being 'part of the job' or a mechanism for ensuring 'how to do the job' and is thus ren-dered invisible (Boud and Middleton 2003). For Lave and Wenger (1991) the concept of a community of practice is an ideal learning context in which new members of the community can engage in 'legitimate peripheral participation' and begin to belong to the community and thus their cultural practices. It is more than simply observing; new community members participate in tasks at increasingly multiple and complex levels. As people participate in communi-ties in practice they move from a position of 'newcomers' to 'old timers' as they become knowledgeable in the practice. It is the subtle opportunities for learning that 'peripheral participation' offers within the 'lived in' world that are crucial.

> It includes an increasing understanding of how, when, and about what old-timers collaborate, collude and collide, and what they enjoy, dislike and respect and admire. In particular it offers exemplars... including masters, finished products and more advanced apprentices in the process of becoming full practitioners.
>
> (Lave and Wenger 2002: 114)

These ideas signify a move away from the developmental theory of Piaget (1972) in that learners acquire structures to understand their world. Lave and Wenger (1991: 47) say, 'Conventional explanations view learning as a process by which a learner internalizes knowledge, whether "discovered," "transmit-ted" from others, or "experienced in interaction" with others'. In this view, knowledge is seen as internal cognitive structures, not social and external in nature. Lave and Wenger (1991) argue there is an apparent lack of recogni-tion in Piaget's work of the role of social influences, which shape the way knowledge is understood, organized, represented and applied. Thus rather than questioning what type of cognitive processes and conceptual structures are involved in learning, they enquire about the kinds of social engagements that provide the proper context for learning to take place (Hanks 1991).

However, the ideas of 'communities of practice' are not without its critics. Contu and Willmott (2003) recognize that communities of practice offer an interesting alternative to understanding learning. Although it is also important to recognize recent popularized perspectives appear to be transgressing away from Lave and Wenger's original view that unequal power relations can mediate opportunities for participation. This is reiterated in later writing by Wenger et al. (2007: 144) in the recognition that a community is not a haven of peace or unbounded goodwill in that they 'have their share of conflicts, jealousies and intrigues'. Contu and Willmott (2003: 12) further argue that Lave and Wenger's ideas need to be revisited and require more of an understanding of how social practices are embedded in history and language. There is a 'danger of assuming a consensus in communities of practice' and further warn of locating practices or behaviour in the context of a unitary community where consensus is not in question. Thus the practice itself is represented as established and relatively unchanging. However, Engeström and Cole (1997) challenge this assumption and argue that knowledge development is ongoing, where collective activity is interlinked with the emergence of novel actions and developing identities of individuals.

Situated learning

At its simplest, situated learning is learning that takes place in the same context in which it is applied. Lave and Wenger (1991: 53) situate learning in communities of practice where 'learning is described as an integral and inseparable aspect of social practice'. To 'situate' learning in social practices challenges the notion that learning is a reaction to teaching. Knowledge is situated within the practices of the community of practice, rather than something which exists 'out there'. Lave and Wenger (1991: 31) argue that situated learning is 'more encompassing in intent than conventional notions of "learning in situ" or "learning by doing" for which it was used as a rough equivalent'. For Seely-Brown and Duguid (1996: 49) this view captures learning 'as part of an inevitably unfinished but continuous process that goes on throughout life. Each event, circumstance, or interaction is not discrete. Rather it is assimilated or appropriated in terms of what has gone on before'.

Therefore what conditions need to be present to be supportive of situated learning? Herrington and Oliver (1995) suggest that any knowledge to be gained needs to be presented in a realistic context, for example, a setting that would normally involve that knowledge. This suggests authentic activities in authentic contexts that reflect the way that knowledge is and will be used in real life need to be available. Learning, to be situated, also requires social interaction and collaboration to enable tacit learning to become explicit. Additionally, processes of modelling and scaffolding by experts needs to be in existence. This form of guidance originates from Vygotsky's (1978) and Rogoff's (1990) ideas of guided participation. This involves joint problem-solving and the gradual withdrawal of the more experienced other as the learner becomes increasingly able to work without close guidance.

While the theories that underpin the notion of Lave and Wenger's concepts of learning are relatively easily explained, implementing these ideas into practice can pose particular problems (Herrington et al. 2004). As part of this chapter, the ideas of communities of practice and situated learning have been applied to a research study involving the development of an online community of practice with mature, part-time higher education students.

Context of the study

As part of a Lifelong Learning Network funded project, in conjunction with two other colleagues, Catherine Lamond and Julie Hughes in the School of Education at Wolverhampton University, we proposed to develop a blended learning model for our foundation degrees in Early Years Services and Supporting Inclusive Practice. The profile of the students undertaking this degree is diverse in terms of age, years of experience of working with children and professional role within the children's workforce. The focus of the project was to aid the progression of level 3 vocational learners through supporting their transition onto level 4 qualifications by developing high quality, innovative, online learning materials for pre-induction and the first year of the foundation degree programmes as well as 'face-to-face' teaching. As part of the project we developed a range of video materials, online learning resources, study skills information and a pre-induction blog that was shared with the students before formal teaching had begun.

The rationale for the introduction of foundation degrees (DfES 2003) is linked to the development of a distinctive qualification as they combine both academic learning with work-based experiences. Thus mature students, usually in employment, are drawn to this kind of part-time study (DfES 2004), where they can 'earn as they learn' (Doyle 2003: 276–277). Similarly, an analysis by the Higher Education Funding Council for England (HEFCE 2007: 57) of entry to higher education for mature students suggested, 'many would not have entered higher education at all without the development of Foundation Degrees'. However, the first year experience of students enrolled on foundation degrees can often be one characterized by insecurity and uncertainty about 'HEness'. Crossan et al. (2003: 57) suggest that mature adults upon entering higher education 'do not easily perceive themselves as a student' and are often initially tentative in their engagement due to limited confidence.

For many foundation degree students, this is their first encounter with studying for a number of years. Thus we wanted to develop a flexible model that eased the transition into higher education and within the project team there was an excitement about the possibilities for learning enhanced by the use of technology. The research was also underpinned by the views of Harvey and Drew (2006: iv) in that foundation degree students are not 'more of the same' and that '[t]here is no first-year experience; there is a multiplicity of first-year experiences'.

For Lave and Wenger (1991) individuals in any community are apprentice learners until they have developed a thorough understanding of what tasks are involved, it is only then they become complete members of the community of practice. To enable students to become aware of the expectations of studying in higher education, as well as their social integration into university life, the idea of a foundation degree as a social learning environment within the context of Lave and Wenger's (1991) communities of practice theory was drawn upon. The project team also held the view that it is through involvement in the social practices of studying for a foundation degree that students' perceived constructs of both their personal and professional identity are shaped. Herrington et al. (2004) argue situated learning and authentic activity is not constrained to learning in real-life places and practice, but that there are critical characteristics of authentic activities that can be incorporated into online learning. The following example illustrates ideas of situated and community learning can be applied to the development of an online community in terms of acquiring knowledge and social practices of studying in higher education.

Developing an online community of practice

The use of a pre-induction blog (Figure 5.1) offered the opportunity for the students to begin to interact online with each other by sharing their thoughts and feelings about starting the course. It also provided the opportunity for course tutors to offer reassurance and provide feed back in relation to queries. This was the first step in the establishment of an online learning community and the beginning of a shift in learning cultures from individual to community learning. For Lave and Wenger (1991) the critical characteristic here would be the value of 'legitimate peripheral practice' that is allowed. Wenger (1998) has written further about features that should be evident in the development of a community of practice. For Wenger (1998), a community exists when sustainable mutual engagement manifests; members begin to negotiate meanings with each other, how they should behave and where systems of support are developed and members can ask for help when needed. It became evident through the interactions of the students through the online blogs that systems of support were being developed.

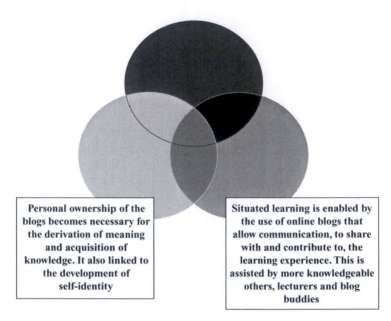

| Personal ownership of the blogs becomes necessary for the derivation of meaning and acquisition of knowledge. It also linked to the development of self-identity | Situated learning is enabled by the use of online blogs that allow communication, to share with and contribute to, the learning experience. This is assisted by more knowledgeable others, lecturers and blog buddies |

Figure 5.1 The use of a pre-induction blog. (Adapted from Mayes and de Freitas 2007)

During the first year of the foundation degree, to develop the sustainability of mutual engagement, small group and large group blogs (Figures 5.2 and 5.3) were utilized. This also helped to develop the students' social integration into university: according to Leung and Kember (2005) the quality of

Online resources

What resources/resource links do you think would be useful to support you in your studies?

Posted by Julie Hughes at 13:28   1 Comment | Post Comment

What other information do you need? Questions you wished that you'd asked

Do you still have questions and queries about your studies? Are there things you'd like to know?

Posted by Julie Hughes at 13:28   10 Comments | Post Comment

How have you found the day so far?

Have there been an highs/lows? Did anything surprise or excite you?

Posted by Julie Hughes at 13:26   11 Comments | Post Comment

What did it feel like coming on to campus this morning?

What were your initial feelings? Have they changed at all?

Posted by Julie Hughes at 13:24   20 Comments, 20 New Comments | Post Comment

Figure 5.2 Example of a pre-induction blog.

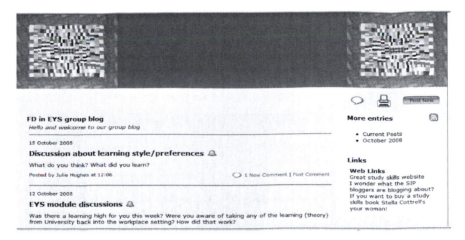

Figure 5.3   Example of a large group blog.

staff–student interactions and relationships with peers and the opportunity to develop a sense of belonging should not be underestimated. The entries into these blogs linked not only to activities associated with their learning on the course, but also social and affective communications between the students and lecturers and students. Wenger (1998: 150) suggests 'engagement in practice gives us certain experiences of participation and what our communities pay attention to reifies us as participants'. Within this project these experiences of participation included how students experience academic, social and cultural inclusiveness. Research by Thomas (2002) of student retention emphasizes this point by identifying the significance of staff–student relationships in terms of learning to know about what studying in higher education is all about. The students' responses in this study indicated that if they felt accepted and valued by lecturing staff through the development of personal relationships, it led to improved outcomes in their self-confidence, motivation and contributed to 'a sense of belonging'. The importance of friendships and mutual support was also identified as a contributory factor in the development of their identity. The opportunity to share concerns, ask questions of each other and debate ideas helped to avoid feelings of inadequacy. Thomas (2002) proposes access to social networks for mature students and collaborative or socially orientated teaching and learning which promoted social relations is vital. It enabled students' to feel confident to ask for help when they needed it from their peers and their lecturers.

In addition to this the project team also utilized the support of 'Blog buddies' where a group of students who had completed their first year were asked to talk online and offer information of their experiences of the foundation

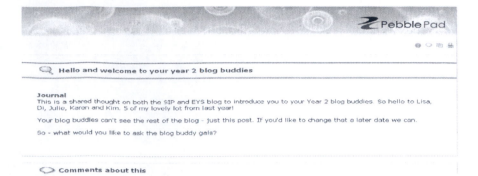

Figure 5.4 Blog buddies.

degree to the new students in year one of the foundation degree (Figure 5.4). This was a key intervention in creating and sustaining a 'buddying' culture. It also relates to Wenger's more recent refinement of his ideas of situated learning in the way in which communities of practice continually reproduce themselves by social learning, so that they develop over time (Wenger et al. 2007).

The use of the blogs in different contexts provided an infrastructure for powerful community learning. This links to Lave and Wenger's ideas that learning involves interactions between novices (students) and more capable and knowledgeable individuals (lecturers), thus indicating an apprentice model of learning. The 'situatedness' of the learning was inherent in the context of the blogs. Within the blog, the students presented diverse demands and competence levels; however, within this online community the students were able to 'make use' of each other. This was particularly evident in the use of 'blog buddies'. As Hung and Der-Thanq (2001: 7) suggest, 'when learning is embedded in rich situations and social constructive acts where meanings can be made sense in the contexts of application and use, learners pick up implicit and explicit knowledge'.

Lave and Wenger (1991) suggest for any community of practice to be successful there need to be 'joint aims'. There needs to be a common purpose for participants to join together, such as shared interests or a commonality of problems. The large group blog provided the opportunity for the students to share their concerns, hopes and expectations of the course initially. However, as the year progressed the students began to use the blog as a source of support both in their academic learning and personal needs. Thus, not only did the students have access to more 'experienced individuals' but also they were able to gradually acquire knowledge of the practice moving from 'peripheral participation to central participation' (Hung and Der-Thanq 2001: 4), in this case, studying in higher education.

Conclusion

Within this chapter, I have explored some of the key ideas relating to Lave and Wenger's principles of developing a community of practice and situated learning. It provides a framework for exploring learning in social circumstances and relating this to a research project has been helpful in showing how theory can be related to a practical situation. Lave and Wenger (1991) suggest that the establishment of a successful community is reliant on several factors, including designing organizational structures that recognize the importance of informal learning, recognition of the importance of participation and communication and developing methods of linking different communities together through shared dialogues and coordination of different practices. The use of the online blogs for part-time early years foundation degree students involved a range of community-building strategies. The role of the lecturers and blog buddies was crucial in facilitating and supporting the community in terms of enabling transparency of practices in higher education, resolving problems and continual monitoring of learning experiences.

It was evident as the community developed the students moved from the periphery of the community to its centre; they became more active and engaged within the culture, eventually assuming the role of an expert. In this there was also a concern with the students' own constructs of their self-identity, with learning to speak, act and improvise in ways that made sense in the community. This was particularly apparent in the development of their professional identity. The use of authentic learning experiences via the blogs provided a context for critical reflection and discussion in terms of their learning on the degree and the opportunity to redefine their professional role in the light of this new learning.

The opportunity for access to mature forms of practice was apparent in enabling 'newcomers' to become more knowledgeable of social and cultural practices. There was very little evidence of what Wenger et al. (2007) refer to as the 'temptation of ownership' and 'imperialism' in the development of the online community. According to Wenger et al. (2007: 142) 'when a community's hold on its domain becomes exclusive, outsiders are likely to feel hostage to the self righteous expertise of specialists'.

Warmington (2004) acknowledges that the development of a 'community' requires a high level of agreement among members in the formation and safeguarding of a shared vision of practice. What was evident from blog entries made by the students was that the nature of the community was constantly changing with different students from different professional pathways connecting and interacting with each other; this was in response to the changing needs of the students with the community. This could have impacted on the community in terms of disparity.

Also, in regards to the development of individual identity, Billett (1994: 13) notes a word of caution in that 'because socio-cultural theorists have a key interest in social and culturally derived knowledge, they may not give due acknowledgment to the individual and idiosyncratic nature of knowledge construction'. It was evident that there were different levels of participation by the students in the online community; this was due to hesitancy about using technology, a lack of confidence in becoming a higher education student, or difficulty in reconciling their engagement in different communities. If we, as the project team did, recognize that learning involves socially organized activity, we perhaps needed to think more carefully about the social activities we provided to ensure all may participate to the full. These activities may involve problem-solving opportunities and seeking experience of new situations from each other, discussing new developments and the sharing of materials.

There was no doubt that the use of the blogs in different contexts provided an arena for powerful peer and community learning; although it was found that it is far easier to talk about situated learning but sustaining interactions and learning together takes time and concentrated effort. However, when reflecting on the outcomes of this project, the development of an online community of practice was a worthwhile experience and one which is being continuously developed by the project team for future students.

Suggested further reading

Hughes, J., Jewson, N. and Unwin, L. (eds) (2007) *Communities of Practice: Critical perspectives*. London: Routledge.
Kimble, C. (2008) *Communities of Practice: Creating learning environments for educators*. Charlotte, NC: Information Age.
Wenger, E., White, N. and Smith, J.D. (2009) *Digital Habitats: Stewarding technology for communities*. Portland, OR: CPSquare.

References

Anning, A. and Edwards, A. (2006) *Promoting Children's Learning from Birth to Five: Developing the new early years professional*, 2nd edn. Maidenhead: Open University Press.
Billett, S. (1994) 'Situated learning: Reconciling culture and cognition.' In *(re)Forming Post-compulsory Education and Training: Conference Proceedings*, Brisbane, Australia, 7–9 December.
Boud, D. and Middleton, H. (2003) 'Learning from others at work.' *Journal of Workplace Learning*, 5(3): 194–202.
Bruner, J. (1999) 'Culture, mind and education.' In B. Moon and P. Murphy (eds) *Curriculum in Context*. London: Paul Chapman.

Contu, A. and Wilmott, H. (2003) 'Re-embedding situatedness: The importance of power relations in learning theory.' *Organization Science*, 14(3): 283–296.

Crossan, B., Field, J., Gallacher, J. and Merrill, B. (2003) 'Understanding participation in learning for non-traditional adult learners: Learning careers and the construction of learning identities.' *British Journal of Sociology of Education*, 24(1): 55–67.

Daniels, H. (2001) *Vygotsky and Pedagogy*. London: RoutledgeFalmer.

Department for Education and Skills (DfES) (2003) *Widening Participation in Higher Education*. Nottingham: DfES.

Department for Education and Skills (DfES) (2004) *Foundation Degree Task Force Report to Ministers*. Nottingham: DfES.

Department for Education and Skills (DfES) (2005) *Children's Workforce Strategy*. Nottingham: DfES.

Doyle, M. (2003) 'Discourses of employability and empowerment: Foundation degrees and the third way discursive repertoires.' *Discourse*, 24: 275–288.

Dunne, L., Goddard, G. and Woolhouse, C. (2008) 'Mapping the changes: A critical exploration into the career trajectories of teaching assistants who undertake a foundation degree'. *Journal of Vocational Education and Training*, 60(1): 49–59.

Engeström, Y. and Cole, M. (1997) 'Situated cognition in search of an agenda.' In D. Kirshner and J.A. Whitson (eds) *Situated Cognition: Social, semiotic, and psychological perspectives*. Mahwah, NJ: Lawrence Erlbaum Associates.

Hanks, W.F. (1991) 'Foreword.' In J. Lave and E. Wenger (eds) *Situated Learning: Legitimate peripheral participation*. Cambridge: Cambridge University Press.

Harvey, L. and Drew, S. with Smith, M. (2006) *The First Year Experience: A literature review for the Higher Education Academy*. York: Higher Education Academy.

Herrington, J. and Oliver, R. (1995) 'Critical characteristics of situated learning: Implications for the instructional design of multimedia.' In J. Pearce and A. Ellis (eds) *Learning with Technology*. Parkville, Vic: University of Melbourne. Available at www.ascilite.org.au/conferences/melbourne95/smtu/papers/herrington.pdf (accessed 11 December 2009).

Herrington, J., Reeves, T.C., Oliver, R. and Woo, Y. (2004) 'Designing authentic activities in web-based courses.' *Journal of Computing in Higher Education*, 16(1): 3–29.

Higher Education Funding Council for England (HEFCE) (2007) *Foundation Degrees: Key statistics 2001–2 to 2006–7*. Available at www.hefce.ac.uk/pubs/hefce2007/07/03 (accessed 1 May 2010).

Hung, D.W.L. and Der-Thanq, C. (2001) 'Situated cognition, Vygotskian thought and learning from the communities of practice perspective: Implications for the design of web-based e-learning.' *Educational Media International*, 38(1): 3–12.

Kember, D. and Leung, D.Y.P. (2004) 'Relationship between the employment of coping mechanisms and a sense of belonging for part time students.' *Educational Psychology*, 24(3): 345–357.

Lave, J. and Wenger, E. (1991) *Situated Learning: Legitimate peripheral participation.* Cambridge: Cambridge University Press.

Lave J. and Wenger, E. (2002) 'Legitimate peripheral participation in communities in practice.' In R. Harrison, F. Reeve, A. Hanson and J. Clarke (eds) *Supporting Lifelong Learning: Perspectives on learning.* London: RoutledgeFalmer.

Leung, D.Y.P. and Kember, D. (2005) 'The influence of the part-time study experience on the development of generic capabilities.' *Journal of Further and Higher Education*, 29(2): 91–101.

Mayes, T. and de Freitas, S. (2007) 'Learning and e-learning: The role of theory.' In H. Beetham and R. Sharpe (eds) *Rethinking Pedagogy for a Digital Age: Designing and delivering e-learning.* London: Routledge.

Penketh, C. and Goddard, G. (2008) 'Students in transition: Mature women students moving from Foundation Degree to Honours level 6.' *Research in Post-Compulsory Education*, 13(3): 315–327.

Piaget, J. (1972) *The Psychology of the Child.* New York: Basic Books.

Rogoff, B. (1990) *Apprenticeship in Thinking: Cognitive development in social context.* New York: Oxford University Press.

Seely-Brown, J. and Duguid, P. (1996) 'Stolen knowledge.' In H. McLellan (ed.) *Situated Learning Perspectives.* Englewood Cliffs, NJ: Educational Technology Publications.

Thomas, L. (2002) 'Student retention in higher education: The role of institutional habitus.' *Journal of Education Policy*, 17(4): 423–442.

Vygotsky, L. (1968) *Thought and Language.* Cambridge, MA: MIT Press.

Warmington, P. (2004) 'Conceptualising professional learning for multi-agency working and user engagement.' Paper delivered at the British Educational Research Association Annual Conference, University of Warwick, 3 September.

Wenger, E. (1998) *Communities of Practice: Learning, meaning and identity.* Cambridge: Cambridge University Press.

Wenger, E. (2000) 'Communities and practice and social learning systems.' *Organization*, 7(2): 225–246.

Wenger, E., McDermott, R. and Synder, W.M. (2007) *Cultivating Communities of Practice.* Boston, MA: Harvard Business School Press.

Worsley, J. (2007) 'Exploring the perspectives of early years practitioners in a newly established children's centre.' In I. Siraj-Blatchford, K. Clarke and M. Needham (eds) *The Team around the Child: Multi-agency working in the early years.* Stoke-on-Trent: Trentham Books.

6 Developing learning dispositions for life

Liz Brooker

Introduction

The idea of 'learning dispositions' is one of the newest and most powerful theoretical constellations to be found in early childhood education. It is an idea which appeared to emerge from nowhere, in the early 1990s, and which then took hold with great speed, influencing the thinking which informs research and practice with both school and preschool children, nationally and internationally. By 2010, in England and the English-speaking world, it has become a commonplace and common-sense notion, part of the everyday language of early educators and of our shared understanding of young children's learning behaviours in settings. Curriculum frameworks, such as the Early Years Foundation Stage in England (DCSF 2008) and Te Whāriki in New Zealand (Ministry of Education (MoE) 1996), affirm the importance of dispositions in shaping children's development and learning from birth and throughout the school years; and practitioners everywhere now recognize the importance of children's attitudes and motivation for their learning. The widely accepted view that children's dispositions, rather than their 'knowledge and skills', may shape their outcomes could be said to have revolutionized early years practice, even if the acceptance of this view within mainstream schooling will take much longer.

This chapter begins by looking at the prehistory of theories of dispositions – the period before the term became a key idea in early education – to identify the two opposing viewpoints from which the idea developed, and the contribution which each of these viewpoints (the psychological and the sociological) has made to our current understandings. It then considers the ways that early childhood educators have adopted and adapted these ideas, including the recent emergence of dispositions theories from a sociocultural perspective. It argues that these latest understandings offer the most positive means to promote both children's wellbeing in the present, and their potential for future success and fulfilment. The last section of the chapter offers examples of children displaying their dispositions through their interactions with the environment of early childhood settings. But first it is necessary to define our terms.

Defining dispositions

Perhaps it is because dispositions theories have their roots in such disparate academic disciplines that the task of defining them in relation to early childhood education can seem problematic. Lilian Katz (1995) was one of the first scholars to deliberate (at some length) on the relationship between this and associated terms such as *habits, traits, attitudes, tendencies, predispositions* and *learning styles* which had been applied by psychologists to children's as well as adults' learning behaviours. Katz's work builds on that of American developmental psychologists (Dweck and Leggett 1988; Dweck 1991) who have studied the range of dispositions children display when they are faced with classroom tasks. She argues that the responses of any individual child to a new task are always likely to follow a similar pattern, and her principal formulation, which has been widely adopted, states that: 'A disposition is a tendency to exhibit frequently, consciously, and voluntarily a pattern of behaviour that is directed towards a broad goal' (Katz 1993: 1).

This definition, however, provokes important questions: first, where do these patterns of behaviour, or dispositions, come from – how do children acquire them? Second, and more importantly for educators – can they be changed? In other words, are children stuck with the dispositions, positive or negative, that they are born with or enter school with, or is there something which educators can do to enable all children to acquire positive dispositions? These questions are of concern to both educators and researchers.

Before pursuing them we can consider an entirely different source for the current focus on dispositions, from the field of social theory. The French sociologist Pierre Bourdieu (Bourdieu and Passeron 1977; Bourdieu and Wacquant 1992), in his efforts to explain the persistence of social inequalities in advanced societies, proposed the term *habitus* as a description for a similar behavioural pattern: the tendency for an individual to behave in a certain way in response to experiences, including educational experiences. Bourdieu explained that his use of the term meant more than simply 'habits', referring rather to a 'system of dispositions towards learning', acquired by the child in its earliest years at home and persisting 'durably' though not unchangeably, through life. These 'dispositions' were the product not simply of the child's innate psychological make-up, or of early experiences of caregiving, but were derived at least in part from the collective *habitus* of the family and community: from their location in society, their social status and esteem, and their capacity to succeed or fail within the 'fields of power' which structured their lives. As Bourdieu (1990: 13) explains, 'these are acquired, socially constituted dispositions', which children carry with them from home to school. For Bourdieu, writing from within a rigid and elitist French system, social class was at the root of many aspects of the *habitus,* but subsequent researchers using this concept (Comber 2000; Brooker 2002; Connolly et al. 2009) have found a variety of sources of explanation for individual children's *habitus* or dispositions. As in the case of psychological explanations for behavioural patterns, what matters for educators is the extent to which dispositions which have negative consequences for children can be overturned by positive educational experiences.

Other familiar ways of talking about dispositions refer more explicitly to the mind and mental behaviours, either by promoting *thinking skills* (Perkins et al. 1993; Claxton 2008) or by focusing on *habits of mind* (Katz 1988; MoE 1996). All these authors however are concerned with the way that *thought* is transformed into *action,* and so each of these approaches supports the intention of developing classroom practices to promote positive dispositions.

Where do dispositions come from?

There is an increasing consensus that all children are born equipped with the positive dispositions which support early learning, and that they are 'hard-wired' to learn through experience (Blakemore and Frith 2005). Katz (2001) explains, in an interview which discusses 'children as scientists':

> Children, all children, are born with the disposition to make sense of their experiences. This is also what scientists do – make sense of experiences by experimenting, by utilizing the scientific process. You can see this disposition even in babies. A 4-month old will drop a spoon and watch as Grandma picks it up – over and over again. She is a scientist, testing her environment to see what happens.
>
> (Katz 2001)

Katz (2001) goes on to say: 'Our job, as adults who work with young children, is to make sure that we do not damage this disposition', but there is some evidence that the 'damage' occurs, for some children, before they encounter professional educators and caregivers.

Developmental psychologists have developed a range of explanations for the dispositions children have acquired before entering school or preschool (Dweck 1991). The most comprehensive of these (Dweck and Leggett 1988) identifies links between children's *behaviour* in response to tasks and activities (their learning approach) and their *beliefs* about themselves as learners (their

Table 6.1   Theories of intelligence, motivational goals and learning approaches

Theories of intelligence	Motivational goals	Learning approach
Entity theory: intelligence is fixed and immutable	Performance goals: aim is to 'prove' ability	Helpless: avoid challenge, avoid failure
Incremental theory: intelligence is mutable and can be improved	Learning goals: aim is to 'improve' ability	Mastery: engage with challenge, risk failure

motivational goals), which in turn reflect their *theories* of intelligence. The links are set out, in a simplified form, in Table 6.1, where the right-hand column shows the behavioural outcomes of dispositions ('helpless' or 'mastery' approaches to learning), the middle column shows the motivational goals which precede such approaches ('performance' or 'learning' goals), and the left-hand column shows the 'theory of intelligence' which underlies these goals.

Put very simply, Dweck's investigations suggest that:

- Children with an 'entity theory' of intelligence, who have acquired the belief that intelligence is innate – some children are just cleverer than others – are likely to develop performance goals, that is, they behave in ways which try to prove to others and themselves that they are clever and capable. As a result, when faced with new challenges, they display a 'helpless' disposition which justifies them in avoiding tasks which may result in failure.
- Children with an 'incremental' theory of intelligence (but with identical levels of measured ability to 'helpless' children) who have acquired the belief that you can become more clever by trying hard or making an effort, are likely to develop goals for improving their ability – 'learning goals' – and as a result tend to attempt new tasks and activities because these are opportunities to get better, to 'master' new knowledge and skills.

In actuality, most children's approach falls somewhere between the two.

Although these studies appear to imply that children's tendency to certain patterns of behaviour has been imprinted on them by the time they begin school, many studies (discussed in Carr 2001) suggest that the learning environments children encounter can transform their negative image of themselves as learners before they have begun to be labelled through formal assessments, which may lead to them labelling themselves as good or bad learners. The role of assessment itself in this process is one we will return to.

As indicated above, Bourdieu's theory of habitus also leaves room for the system of dispositions, developed by every individual through early experience, to change as he or she travels through the education system, in response to new experiences:

> The habitus acquired in the family is at the basis of the structuring of school experiences . . . the habitus transformed by the action of the school, itself diversified, is in turn at the basis of all subsequent experiences . . . and so on from restructuring to restructuring.
> (Bourdieu and Wacquant 1992: 134n)

In other words, although an individual never loses the dispositions which were laid down by early experiences, these dispositions may be modified as a result of each new opportunity offered by educators: the children of marginalized families and communities may start out with poor estimations of their prospects, but these estimations can be changed by teachers. Helpfully, the psychologists and social theorists are in agreement on this point.

Dispositions in the early childhood classroom

The association between dispositions (children's theories and patterns of motivation) and early education (children's experiences of professional care) was first made in the early 1990s, when researchers studied the short-term and long-term outcomes of early education, particularly on children from poor communities. Kathy Sylva, in a series of landmark writings which have influenced policy and practice in the UK and elsewhere (Sylva 1994a, 1994b), examined the outcomes from programmes such as High/Scope which deliberately developed children's awareness of themselves as learners. Like Lilian Katz (1995), she identified the development of positive dispositions towards learning as the most important outcome of early education – an outcome which programmes such as High/Scope, which involved children in articulating their plans for activity, and reviewing the successful implementation of those plans, were found to support. Children's long-term outcomes, therefore, are understood to be the responsibility of policymakers, programme-providers and educators, as well as parents.

Both Katz (1995) and Sylva (1994b) emphasize the importance of supporting learning dispositions, rather than focusing on knowledge and skills, in developing early childhood curricula. Sylva's (1994b) evaluation of the impact of early education concludes that:

> The most important impact of early education appears to be on children's aspirations, motivations and school commitment. These are

> moulded through experiences in the pre-school classroom which en-
> able children to enter school with a positive outlook and begin a
> school career of commitment and social responsibility.
>
> (Sylva 1994b: 91)

Children's 'positive outlook' includes both a sense of personal self-efficacy, and a sense of social commitment. The first of these is associated with the theories of intelligence, and the view of the self as a learner, described in Dweck's work. The second is strongly associated with the arguments of sociocultural theorists, which are discussed in the next section.

Katz (1995) meanwhile addressed the practical issues facing educators: which 'school' or preschool practices, undertaken in good faith by educators, might be responsible for extinguishing children's innate dispositions to learn, and which practices might help to sustain and support their motivation? Her answers to these questions are offered as 'Seven reasons for focusing on dispositions' (Katz 1995: 63–66), and emphasize that early formal learning, though effective in conveying knowledge and skills, is likely to be antithetical to the development of positive dispositions. The acquisition of knowledge and skills, she points out, does not mean that they will be used and applied (listening skills do not make children listen; reading skills do not make children read). Instructional processes designed to *teach* skills may undermine the disposition to use those skills (drill in reading may not produce readers, but may instead discourage reading). And dispositions are best learned when they are

> modelled for children by those around them – by teachers who think
> aloud about their uncertainties and their problem-solving. If teachers
> want their young pupils to have robust dispositions to investigate,
> hypothesize, experiment, and so forth, they might consider making
> their own such intellectual dispositions more visible to the children.
>
> (Katz 1995: 65)

Katz's thinking led her to sponsor the 'project method' (Katz and Chard 2000) which became associated with the methods of the Reggio Emilia pre-primary schools, and her subsequent writings have developed these ideas further. She explains the importance of such methods in response to an interview question:

> I define 'project' as an in-depth investigation of a phenomenon or
> an event in children's own experience or environment that is worth
> learning about -something children are interested in, something they
> can readily observe and interact with. During project work, we help
> children formulate their own research questions, figure out ways
> to find the answers, and assist them in representing their findings.

> Worthwhile projects contribute to children's confidence in their own experiences and help them understand those experiences more fully.
>
> (Katz 2001)

The principle of working with children's individual and collective interests informs the most recent, sociocultural, strand of theorizing about dispositions.

Dispositions as social and situated

Since the 1970s, as Vygotskian and post-Vygotskian theorizing has proliferated (Wells and Claxton 2001) (see Chapter 1), sociocultural approaches to development and learning have prompted the rethinking of all aspects of early childhood education. This rethinking applies also to the study of dispositions. Where dispositions had once been understood as an attribute or characteristic of an individual, and in part innate, in recent years they have been recognized as the product of experiences which are socially situated: in the case of preschool children, of experiences generated by the ethos and practice of the preschool educators. These dispositional 'outcomes' may in addition be both temporary and context-dependent, as children demonstrate different characteristics at different times, in different environments, and with different companions. And rather than simply being structured by the environment, they may be simultaneously structuring that environment, and in turn transforming the impact of that environment on others.

'Learning dispositions', in other words, are now seen to be inextricably connected with 'learning places', or 'dispositional milieux' (Carr 2001), and this recognition opens them up, to a far greater extent, for investigation and interpretation. The dispositions in question, though observed and identified in an individual child, are seen to be associated with that child's social identity, and with the identities which are made possible in the group of which the child is a member. And the behaviours which result from these dispositions, making them visible to observers, are not behaviours which occur in isolation, but are functions of the artefacts and activities which constitute the child's environment. These complex relationships need some unpacking.

Margaret Carr, who has led this rethinking, has described the process by which she came to conceptualize 'learning dispositions' (Carr 2001: 5). To the 'knowledge and skills' which, as Katz has claimed, are often seen as the core content of early childhood curriculum, she first adds the notion of 'intent', to arrive at the concept of *learning strategies*. These in turn, by the further addition of the 'social partners and practices and tools' available in the environment, become *situated strategies*. Finally, through the addition of 'motivation', we arrive at the concept of *learning dispositions*. Any disposition which a child displays, in other words, is the visible product of a relationship between factors in the child and factors in the environment, which may include play partners, practitioners, artefacts, activities, routines and the forms of relationship which the setting promotes.

'Motivation' however remains a key element in this complex formulation, because a child demonstrating positive learning dispositions is one who can be described as *ready, willing and able*. These three terms too are carefully distinguished, and are always situated. They describe a child who at any moment in time:

- Sees him/herself as a learner (and hence is *ready* to undertake new tasks and activities)
- Sees this as a place to learn (and hence is *willing* to undertake these tasks and activities)
- Possesses the necessary knowledge and skills to learn (and hence is *able* to undertake these tasks and activities).

As Carr (2001) points out, readiness (seeing oneself as a learner) describes one of the social identities which may be available to a child, and which we would expect to be fostered in a good preschool environment. Children in preschools may have many identities available to them: 'one of the [noisy] boys' or 'one of the [tidy] girls', one of the new children or one of the older ones, one of the good children or one of the naughty ones, one of the best at climbing or one of the best at drawing. But if preschool is to promote positive learning dispositions, *all* children must come to see themselves as learners, and for this to happen there must be critical reflection and conscious planning by educators, directed at creating a community of learners. In Katz's words, this is a matter which 'deserves serious attention in the course of curriculum planning and teacher education' (Katz 1995: 66).

Assessing dispositions-in-action: making learning visible

Within the Te Whāriki curriculum, positive dispositions are related to the notion of *mana*, a Maori word roughly translated as 'self-respect, prestige, power, strength and esteem', and hence related to the self-image of the 'mastery learner' described by Dweck (1991). One of the curriculum principles, *whakamana*, is a commitment to empowerment, which means offering all children the opportunity to acquire such *mana*: 'The early childhood curriculum empowers the child to learn and grow' (MoE 1996: 40). And one of the most important means to this end is the practice of assessment, by means of learning stories which document and reify the child's dispositions, making her or his learning visible.

In order to assess what is really occurring in the child's growth as a learner, rather than the possibly trivial by-products of children's activities, learning stories draw out from their narratives the dispositions which children display. The five rather abstract strands of the Te Whāriki curriculum are conceived as icebergs whose visible 'peaks' are the dispositions-in-action which a practitioner is able to observe as the child participates in activities and forms relationships. These are described as:

- Taking an interest
- Being involved
- Persisting with difficulty or uncertainty
- Communicating with others
- Taking responsibility.

Adults in the setting reflect together on their written narratives, and reflect them back to the child and family, informing the child of the dispositions he or she has displayed, and commenting on their new learning. In one example, Carr (2005: 5) describes a child who 'hones' his learning dispositions over a period of months, by bringing his prior learning (about the natural world, and about researching unfamiliar topics) together with his more recent interests, when he becomes interested in an unusual bone found on the beach. She shows the child, Leo, building on his existing abilities as a learner by: 'widening an interest, recognising that learners are uncertain and frequently wrong, adding some interesting strategies for persevering with finding information, becoming able to use a new communication tool, and sharing responsibility for learning with the teacher'. In doing so he is developing *working theories*, another important aspect of being a learner.

Leo's development is not solely the product of his *readiness*, his own sense of himself as a learner, although it is clear that his teachers have supported this quality through their close commentary on his learning. It depends too on his *willingness*, his knowledge that this is an appropriate place to be undertaking an inquiry. This brings us back to Carr's idea of a 'dispositional milieu', or 'learning place'.

> Learning occurs in learning places . . .
> The effects of early childhood experiences are the result of complex interactions between the learner and the learning place, between learning dispositions and a dispositional milieu
> (Carr 2001: 35, 42)

Learning dispositions are supported, and can be observed, in places where the artefacts, activities and social partners on offer are conducive to learning. Leo might have been less willing to try out his ideas, and persist with his uncertainties, if he found himself in a learning place which valued correct answers above speculation, and where the teacher's learning intentions took priority over the child's interests. He might equally have abandoned his quest for knowledge if he found himself in conversation with a teacher who 'knew all the answers' and provided them for him; or if his preschool was one in which 'being a boy' implied engaging in continuous rough-and-tumble or avoidance of the artefacts and activities which support cognitive learning. As it was, his behaviour showed a 'willingness' which indicated that he knew himself to be in a 'learning place'.

The final aspect of Leo's learning disposition – being able – is supported by the opportunity he has to draw on the knowledge and skills provided by his own interest and by his home and community experiences, as well as on the learning resources of the preschool environment (where he is helped to email a photograph of the mystery bone fragment to a local museum). Building on children's prior knowledge and interests is a further means to support the development of positive dispositions.

Funds of knowledge and children's interests

Research into dispositions – from Bourdieu's work to the present – has shown up some of the negative, as well as positive, learning environments which children may encounter as they enter the education system, and which contribute to sustaining, enhancing or extinguishing the learning dispositions which they will carry with them into later life. One of the most widespread concerns has been about the 'funds of knowledge' (Moll et al. 1992; Hedges 2010) which children acquire in their early learning outside the home, but which are not always reflected in the preschool or school curriculum.

Children's early 'home knowledge' begins with their language (or dialect, or accent) and extends into the forms of relationships they encounter and the styles of learning they are offered as well as including the factual knowledge and the practised skills which form part of their daily lives. Cross-cultural studies (Rogoff 1990, 2003) have demonstrated convincingly that all children acquire such knowledge, through the guided participation offered by those around them as well as by the 'tacit arrangements' of their environment, and so all can be assumed to be relatively well versed in the expertise which is valued in their home culture as they enter their first educational settings. Studies of transitions (Comber 2000; Brooker 2002) have focused attention on the ways that this 'home knowledge' transfers – or does not – into school environments where completely different types of knowledge and skills may be valued.

Both Comber (2000) and Brooker (2002) adopt the analytic tools supplied by Bourdieu to identify the *habitus* of the case study children they observe, and the *cultural capital*, acquired in the home, which each of them brings in to school. Comber's children, in an Australian classroom, respond in different ways to the learning opportunities in the classroom because they have different experiences, and expectations, of the kinds of help adults give and the kinds of behaviour which are appropriate. But children's differing classroom behaviours may set up a 'feedback loop', prompting different levels of input from teachers and inequitable opportunities to access the curriculum. Teachers too have dispositions, and need to sustain their own sense of self-esteem and professionalism through their relationships with all the children in their care.

A study by Hedges (2010) offers further analysis of the ways in which children's funds of knowledge, from outside the home, support the interests which they bring to school and invest in the activities of the preschool classroom. A teacher in her case study assumes, quite naturally, that the children's engagement with classroom activities such as sand play demonstrates their enthusiasm for these activities, whereas Hedges' own observations and discussions with children and families reveal that children may be acting on entirely different interests and impulses, connected with their lives outside the school. Where children find their existing knowledge, expertise and interests ignored in the classroom, they lack opportunities to both display, and sustain, their positive dispositions towards learning.

Tracking the development of learning dispositions: some examples

Having developed a comprehensive theoretical picture of the nature of young children's dispositions, Carr and Claxton (2002) have explored ways of 'tracking' these dispositions as children develop their participation in the setting. This aspect of their work is of interest both to educators and to researchers, since it reflects the dynamic nature of a sociocultural understanding of dispositions as patterns which change as a result of the child's continuing interactions with people, places and things. For educators, such observations enable thoughtful planning aimed at enhancing the child's participation repertoires, while for researchers, including teacher-researchers, they help to avoid the labelling of children which may result from a static understanding.

Claxton and Carr (2004: 89–90) argue that a 'learning curriculum' should seek to strengthen three different dimensions of children's dispositions: by making them more *robust,* by increasing their *breadth,* and by enhancing their *richness*. Some small examples of children's behaviour may demonstrate the application of these terms.

Case study 6.1: Benji (16 months, in day-care)

19 September

Children are still arriving in the morning as Benji begins a leisurely, calm and self-possessed exploration of the nursery area. He stops and stands for some time watching Hana (13 months), who is shrieking in protest at her father's recent departure, but then appears to have made a sudden decision to act. He goes to select an interesting object for himself: a colourful small teddy in trousers. Benji plays with the top of the trouser-zip and gazes happily at the teddy, waving it from side to side and admiring it. Then he walks towards Hana and offers it to her, holding it close to her face. Hana doesn't see it at once so he brings it even closer, clearly 'giving' it to her. Hana however is upset and angry, and bats the teddy away roughly with her arm so it falls on the floor. Benji picks it up and tries again, attempting to explain verbally that this is a gift. Hana's key worker thanks Benji and explains that Hana doesn't want it at present.

> *Taking an interest*
> *Being involved*
> *Taking responsibility*
> *Communicating with others*
> *Persisting with difficulty*

Benji notices Lillian, his key worker, who comes through the door holding a CD and then begins to collect streamers and shakers from a cupboard. Benji begins to jig up and down excitedly in front of Lillian, to show her that he is eager for music time (in an adjoining room) to begin. Lillian understands, and explains to him that he will have to wait while she goes to prepare the room.

> *Taking an interest*
> *Being involved*
> *Communicating with others*

Benji turns away and is invited by another staff member to paint with her: he responds and takes some time to make careful choices of brushes and paints before beginning.

> *Being involved*

In the space of a few minutes, Benji shows many signs of positive dispositions, as listed in the right-hand comment column of this observation. These are not simply qualities *in Benji*, however, but qualities of his interactions with an environment which offers many opportunities to work with people and objects towards desired goals – such as comforting another child, participating in a music group, or commencing a painting. The task of the staff in this centre, as they reflect on Benji's demonstrations of belonging and wellbeing, is to consider how they can help him to become:

- More *robust*, showing positive attitudes consistently and frequently rather than occasionally
- More *broad*, showing them across a wider range of activities and people, such as children from other rooms or new adults in the setting
- More *rich*, demonstrating complexity and subtlety by combining actions (he is already doing this in his efforts with Hana).

The dynamic development of young children's dispositions can be observed over a matter of days, as the second example shows.

Case study 6.2: Hana (13 months, in day-care)

26 September

Lillian leads Hana, who is protesting, into the small room. Hana kneels on the mat and says 'Mummy, Mummy' a few times, but quietly, to Lillian, who invites her to come and meet the 'new baby' (a 9-month-old) who is in the sand area.

On the way to this area, Hana stops and sits on the floor next to Billy (7 months) who has a basket of sounds objects; she squats and then kneels a short distance from Billy, and picks up two metal jar-lids, which she bangs together. She repeats this action with more intention, and interacts teasingly with Billy, who looks at her with interest. She continues to bang, look, tease, turn-take with Billy, and both giggle.	> *Taking an interest* > *Being involved* > *Taking responsibility* > *Communicating with others*
Hana walks away alone. She looks around the room with interest then kneels on a rug to play with a garage, sorting out the cars with seeming contentment.	> *Taking an interest*

At this early stage in her settling, Hana is not displaying all the signs of wellbeing and belonging which her key workers would ideally like to see. But a focus on the positive signs reveals that she is already forming relationships and acquiring routines within which she is able to act independently, to accept support from an adult, or to make a contribution to a younger child's learning. There are clear indications for staff of the ways that her dispositions might be supported across other relationships, artefacts and activities in the setting, to become robust, broad and rich.

Conclusion

The new study of dispositions is an exciting one for both educators and researchers, building on traditional good practice in observing children while avoiding the traditional labelling of children (as shy, bold, confident, tearful) which saw children's qualities as innate – within the child – rather than social – stretched across the social milieu. For adults too, the process of working with dispositions can open doors into other intellectual disciplines, stretching our own understanding and capacities.

Suggested further reading

Claxton, G. and Carr, M. (2004) 'A framework for teaching learning: The dynamics of disposition.' *Early Years*, 24(1): 87–97.
Katz, L.G. (1993) *Dispositions as Educational Goals*. Urbana, IL: ERIC Clearinghouse on Elementary and Early Childhood Education [ED363454]. Available at www.edpsycinteractive.org/files/edoutcomes.html (accessed 17 November 2009).
Sylva, K. (1994) 'The impact of early learning on children's later development (Appendix C)'. In C. Ball (ed.) *Start Right: The importance of early learning*. London: Royal Society of Arts.

References

Blakemore, S.J. and Frith, U. (2005) *The Learning Brain: Lessons for education*. Oxford: Blackwell.
Bourdieu, P. (1990) *In Other Words: Essays towards a reflexive sociology*. Cambridge: Polity.
Bourdieu, P. and Passeron, J-C. (1977) *Reproduction in Education, Society and Culture*. London: Sage.
Bourdieu, P. and Wacquant, L. (1992) *An Introduction to Reflexive Sociology*. Cambridge: Polity.
Brooker, L. (2002) *Starting School: Young children learning cultures*. Maidenhead: Open University Press.

Carr, M. (2001) *Assessment in Early Childhood Settings: Learning stories*. London: Paul Chapman.

Carr, M. (2005) 'Learning dispositions in early childhood and key competencies in school: A new continuity?' Paper presented at the New Zealand Educational Institute (NZEI) Early Years Conference, Hamilton, New Zealand, 22 April.

Carr, M. and Claxton, G. (2002) 'Tracking the development of learning dispositions.' *Assessment in Education*, 9(1): 9–37.

Claxton, G. (2008) *Learning to Learn: A key goal in a 21ˢᵗ century curriculum. Futures: Meeting the challenge*. London: Qualifications and Curriculum Authority.

Claxton, G. and Carr, M. (2004) 'A framework for teaching learning: The dynamics of disposition.' *Early Years*, 24(1): 87–97.

Comber, B. (2000) 'What really counts in early literacy lessons?' *Language Arts*, 78(1): 39–49.

Connolly, P., Kelly, B. and Smith, A. (2009) 'Ethnic habitus and young children: A case study in Northern Ireland.' *European Early Childhood Education Research Journal*, 17(2): 217–232.

Department for Children, Schools and Families (DCSF) (2008) *Early Years Foundation Stage*. Nottingham: DCSF.

Dweck, C. (1991) *Self-theories: Impact on motivation, personality and development*. Philadelphia, PA: Taylor & Francis.

Dweck, C. and Leggett, C. (1988) 'A socio-cognitive approach to motivation and achievement.' *Psychological Review*, 95: 256–273.

Hedges, H. (2010) 'Whose goals and interests? The interface of children's play and teachers' pedagogical practices.' In L. Brooker and S. Edwards (eds) *Engaging Play*. Maidenhead: McGraw-Hill.

Katz, L.G. (1988) 'What should young children be doing?' *American Educator*, 12(2): 28–33, 44–45.

Katz, L.G. (1993) *Dispositions as Educational Goals*. Urbana, IL: ERIC Clearinghouse on Elementary and Early Childhood Education [ED363454]. Available at www.edpsycinteractive.org/files/edoutcomes.html (accessed 17 November 2009).

Katz, L.G. (1995) *Talks with Teachers of Young Children: A collection*. Norwood, NJ: Ablex. (ERIC Document No. ED380232)

Katz, L.G. (2001) Interview in *Early Childhood Today*. Available at www2.scholastic.com/browse/article.jsp?id=3746007 (accessed 17 November 2009).

Katz, L.G. and Chard, S.C. (2000) *Engaging Children's Minds: The project approach*. Norwood, NJ: Ablex.

Ministry of Education (MoE) (1996) *Te Whāriki*. Wellington, NZ: Learning Media.

Moll, L.C., Amanti, C., Neff, D. and Gonzalez, N. (1992) 'Funds of knowledge for teaching: Using a qualitative approach to connect homes and classrooms.' *Theory into Practice*, 31(2): 132–141.

Perkins, D.N., Jay, E. and Tishman, S. (1993) 'Beyond abilities: A dispositional theory of thinking.' *Merrill-Palmer Quarterly*, 39: 1–21.

Rogoff, B. (1990) *Apprenticeship in Thinking: Cognitive Development in Social Context.* Oxford: Oxford University Press.

Rogoff, B. (2003) *The Cultural Nature of Human Development.* Oxford: Oxford University Press.

Sylva, K. (1994a) 'School influences on children's development.' *Journal of Child Psychology and Psychiatry*, 34(1): 135–170.

Sylva, K. (1994b) 'The impact of early learning on children's later development (Appendix C).' In C. Ball (ed.) *Start Right: The importance of early learning.* London: Royal Society of Arts.

Wells, G. and Claxton, G. (eds) (2001) *Learning for Life in the 21st Century.* Oxford: Blackwell.

PART 2
Structure, power and knowledge

7 The sociology of childhood: children's agency and participation in telling their own stories

Tim Waller and Angeliki Bitou

Introduction

This chapter provides an overview of the 'new sociology of childhood' and the concept of childhood as a social construct. A number of powerful ideas have evolved under the conceptual framework of the sociology of childhood. The chapter opens with a discussion of how children are identified as social constructors, 'active in the construction and determination of their own social lives' (James and Prout 1997: 8). Two key concepts are 'agency' and 'participation', which are critically discussed in detail. The chapter reflects on the ongoing debate about power and the role of adults in the social construction of childhood.

The chapter then draws on recent research by the authors in early years settings to provide examples of children's agency and participation in telling their own stories. We conclude by arguing that a key challenge in promoting children's participation is how to ensure children have the space to articulate their views and perspectives beyond the constraints of adult views, interpretation and agenda.

The social construction of childhood

An understanding of childhood as a social construct is a key feature of the 'new sociology of childhood'. As James and Prout (1997: 7) point out, 'the immaturity of children is a biological fact of life but the ways in which this immaturity is understood and made meaningful is a fact of culture'. Views of childhood have changed over time and are changing. In contemporary culture childhood has become a formal category with a social status, and seen as an important stage in development (Waller 2009). As Jenks (1996) has argued, this analysis places 'childhood' within a social construct, rather than a natural phenomenon.

Central to this theory is the recognition of children as social constructors 'active in the construction and determination of their own social lives, of those around them and of the societies in which they live' (James and Prout 1997: 8). Children are capable of both forming and being formed by circumstances and social phenomena (James et al. 1998). This view both acknowledges and gives voice to children as a social group who have 'remained in silence' for a long time (James and Prout 1997: 7). The focus is on children as beings rather than becomings (Qvortrup et al. 1994), experts on their own lives (Clark and Moss 2001) and competent to share their views and opinions (James and Prout 1997).

The sociology of childhood therefore moves far beyond the traditional psychological notion of the child and childhood (James 2005). James argues that popular discourses and predominant theories of each historical period determine the way we view and see the child. A further significant development in our understanding of children and childhood relates to the questioning of a 'normative' and universal childhood for all children across the world and recognition of the plurality of many childhoods (Jenks 1996), which are determined culturally (James et al. 1998) and historically (Qvortrup 2009).

Childhood is therefore not fixed and not universal, it is 'mobile and shifting' (Walkerdine 2004). This means that children experience many different and varied childhoods. There are local variations and global forms, depending on class, 'race', gender, geography, time, etc. (Penn 2005). As Waller (2009) notes, until recently most of the published research and writing about children, childhood and child development has focused on individual development as a natural progress towards adulthood. This natural progress is conceived as the same for all children regardless of class, gender or 'race'. Furthermore, this is a traditional, western developmental view of the child, which is used to categorize all children throughout the world (Dahlberg et al. 2007). Much of this considerable body of work, written from the perspective of psychology and developmental psychology, has promoted what Walkerdine (2004: 107) suggests is an 'essential childhood' (Waller 2009). The new sociology of childhood has therefore been critical of the place of developmental psychology in producing explanations of children as potential subjects, which classify children and their abilities into boxes, according to their age (Corsaro 2005a) and where the child is studied and tested in an 'individual' way (Cannella 1999: 37).

Further, the general view about children and adults as separate social groups assumes discontinuity and a generational demarcation where children are perceived as counterparts to the adults (Olwig and Gulløv 2003). An indicator of the discontinuity between the generations is related to the expectations placed on children in the Early Years Foundation Stage (EYFS) (DfES 2007) in England (see the point above referring to the classification of children). As Frønes (2005: 269) argues, 'the expanding educational system from pre-schools to higher education, illustrates the homogenization of children's life-worlds'. For Frønes, differentiation between adults and children is produced and maintained due to the institutionalization and the structural homogenization of childhood. Thus childhood is described as 'something children do' (Frønes 2005: 270), it is a process where children move forward to the future in contrast with a traditional psychological perspective which assumes children are dependent on their own past.

Two powerful ideas from the new sociology of childhood, which have influenced policy and practice in early childhood education and care, as well as contemporary understanding, are 'agency' and 'participation'. These are now discussed in turn.

Agency

'Agency' involves children's capacity to understand and act upon their world, thus demonstrating competence from birth (James et al. 1998). From this perspective, children are viewed as active agents who construct their own cultures (Corsaro 2005a), have their own activities, their own time and their own space (Qvortrup et al. 1994: 4). It seeks to understand the definitions and meaning children give to their own lives and recognizes children's competence and capacity to understand and act upon their world. However, as Waller (2009) argues, despite the fact children's agency seems to be recognized broadly in the field, there is an ongoing debate about power and the role of adults in the social construction of childhood and the agency of children in their own lives.

The fact that children can express their feelings and emotions in their surroundings, confirms their ability to act competently. Nevertheless, the term 'agency' embeds a more active role (Mayall 2002). Children as agents cannot only express their desires and wishes but also negotiate and interact within their environment causing change.

The phrase 'children are experts on their own lives', which was proposed by Langsted (1994) and developed as a principle in the Mosaic Approach (Clark and Moss 2001, 2005), has recently become popular. However, it is clear that there is an ambivalence about children's agency. In this conception a child is an expert and an adult a novice, thus counter to sociocultural theory which views children and adults as co-constructors of their joint experience (Rogoff 2003). Additionally, this view separates children from the adults' world and positions them in their own places and spaces. Thus, children seem unable to participate in two cultures (peer and adult) at the same time (Corsaro 2005a) while they do not appear to be influenced by the social changes that are happening in the adults' world. Here, Hendrick (1997: 59) makes a critical point about the agency of the child. He argues that changes in the conception of childhood did not just happen, they were contested and not least important among the contestants were the children themselves, but in the context of joint interaction with peers and adults.

Corsaro's (2009) work on researching peer culture is a significant contribution to understanding children's agency and competence. Corsaro (2005a) declares that children's creative role in society is reflected in the fabrication of their own culture and in their contribution to the adults' world. For instance, he asserts that because children infract adult rules, or extend and confer new meanings on the adults' world, this is an indication of their active agency in society. However, James (2005) argues that children and adults perceive childhood in a different way. For children, childhood is a transitory period, whereas for adults it is a stable period even though the members are changing over and over again. According to Qvortrup (2009), children and adults are equal participants and 'social products' in society, bearing in mind that whatever happens in their lives should be seen as a result of social construction and not biological determination. Thus children are not 'consumers' of the culture that adults create, as traditional theories assume, but are indomitable social contributors.

Corsaro (2005a) views the term socialization as problematic because it is embedded the 'dogma' of the isolated individual. He declares that sociology should see children's socialization not under the lens of the individualistic and isolated internalization into adult's society but as a process where children can construct communally and jointly with adults to generate change in society. Thus he recommends the use of the term 'interpretive reproduction' instead of socialization. He explains that 'interpretive' is used to denote the process where children actively retain the information given by adults when they produce their own peer culture in a dynamic way. Children do not just simplify what they have taken from adults but replicate it and participate actively to produce culture and change in society – this is 'reproduction'. Simultaneously the term reproduction conveys that children are already members of society affected by the pre-existing culture, which in turn has been affected by historical changes.

Corsaro's powerful idea has implications for our understanding of pedagogy and practice in early years settings. Corsaro (2005a: 42) argues that children in the early years setting determine their control upon adults' rules through 'secondary adjustment'. The term refers to children's responses to the regulations of the adult's world and they can use secondary adjustment once they perceive membership of a group. Children from the age of 2 years are able to discern between adults and children,

> while young children might lack the cognitive skills to infer the implications of both the embrace of and resistance to organizational rules for personal identity, they do have a clear notion of the importance and restrictiveness of the adult world as compared to children's worlds.
>
> (Corsaro 2003: 141)

Additionally, Corsaro states that through the wrestling between adults' rules and their desires, children manage to determine the constituents of their peer culture. For this reason it is believed children's partnership and involvement in the adult's world is vital in young people's lives.

Corsaro (2005b) contends that Emirbayer and Mische's (1998) definition of agency is particularly valuable as they consider agency as interrelated to time (past, present and future). An example of children's agency in 'telling their own story' drawing on Emirbayer and Mische (1998) is given in Case study 7.1.

Case study 7.1: The sleeping game

Background

The research reported here is part of an ethnographic study that took place over six months as part of a PhD. The setting is a nursery school in Greece belonging to the Day Care Centres of the Organization ΟΡΓΑΝΙΣΜΟΣ ΕΡΓΑΤΙΚΗΣ ΕΣΤΙΑΣ (OEE) where the researcher is a practitioner. The study involved a sample of six children aged 2.5 to 3 years old who were randomly selected. The purpose of the research was to investigate children's involvement in the curriculum and the planning of the curriculum.

Researcher's field notes 11th February

[The children are engaged in "free play" inside the setting]

Eleni and Anastasia take a duvet and a pillow and lie down on the mattress. They cover their body and they pretend they are sleeping. Christos observes what the two girls are doing. It is quiet in the room. He waves to me with his finger. I gesture to indicate to him that I cannot understand what he wants. He indicates to me that it is light switch. "The light?" I ask him, just moving my lips without any noise and he nods to me "yes".

I switch off the light. I was not sure what to do next as I could not see anything and I am worried about the two girls. I switch on the light. The two girls look surprised at me.

Eleni tells me: "Switch it off!!!"

I switch it off.

"Switch it off to sleep!!!" Eleni said again

"Don't switch it on because the bulb will break" Christos tells me from the other side of the table.

Practitioner: "Well we will sit down here at the table to do a small task and then you will play again, actually we will get down for snack time."

"No!!" (Aspasia)

"Yes!!" (Practitioner)

"No!!" (Aspasia)

"Yes! Come here to the table Panayiotis, come here Christos, Eleni, Aspasia, Maria.

I go to switch on the light, following the practitioner's instructions.

"Switch it off!!" (Christos)

All the children were at the table except Eleni and Aspasia. Christos asked me to switch it off. Eleni and Aspasia are still on the mattress lying down. Eleni asked me to switch it off.

"We will switch it off later on!" Come here Eleni to do the task now! (The practitioner answers)

"Shall I turn it on or off?" I ask them.

"Turn it off!" (Aspasia)

"They told me to turn it on because you are about to do a task. . . . I don't know . . . what shall I do?"

"I don't want to!" (Aspasia)

Discussion

In the above case study, which takes places during children's 'free play', the meaning of agency will be examined through Emirbayer and Mische's (1998) model which suggests a reconstructive, temporal process determined by the past, the present and the future. They state that it consists of 'iteration' referring to a habit or an old pattern the individual may have, of 'projectivity' meaning the intention the individual may have to change the old pattern and 'the practical evaluation' pointing to the possible trajectories of action. In the above example with Christos, Aspasia and Eleni, there are two old patterns – the sleeping game (the researcher has observed children many times playing as if they are sleeping and being quiet or re-enacting the sleeping process when they are at home) and the activity at the table which is part of the programme planned daily by the practitioner.

As Corsaro (2005a) and Rogoff (2003) propose, during their engagement in an activity children intend to improve or change an old routine. In Case study 7.1, this intention is clear both in play with peers (Corsaro 2005a) and in their interaction with an adult (Rogoff 2003), contributing in this way to changing the routine. Here Christos watches the two girls play the sleeping game and notices that the only missing element for the girls' game was the light (when we are sleeping the light is off). However, the light was still on. Christos wonders how it would be possible to reach the light switch – only an adult will be able to help him. The practitioner was busy with the preparation of the activity so Christos asked the researcher to achieve his goal. The researcher follows his instructions but thinks that the two girls may be scared and she turns on the light again. It appears that the two girls enjoy playing without the light, while Christos tells the researcher that she should not turn the lights on and off as they are going to break and for this reason they are better being off. Christos' excuse is another old pattern transferring from home to day-care centre. His mother reports that on many occasions she has used the same excuse when she wants to prevent him from using an object.

Participation

Participation is defined here as children's right to participate in processes and decisions that affect their lives. This perspective is informed by both recent theory and policy impacting on early childhood. First, it follows on from the acknowledgement of the significance of children's agency (the sociology of childhood, above) and has also been strongly influenced by the introduction of the United Nations Convention on the Rights of the Child (UNCRC) in 1989. Internationally there is now an overwhelming emphasis on the recognition of children as active citizens with the democratic right to participate as result of the introduction of the UNCRC (Smith 2007). Children's right to participate is typically given consideration in western countries and is a core component of early years policy. For example, in England, following the UNCRC, the Children Act (DfES 2004a) and *Every Child Matters* (DfES 2004b) established the right of the child to be listened to.

Realizing participation in practice, however, requires a commitment to providing appropriate contexts in which children can actively explore options necessary for active participation. As Bae (2009: 391) argues, participation goes beyond mere 'individualistic choice routines'. In this endeavour children's views of their own childhood are particularly significant (Waller 2009) and an important aspect is children's own views of their daily experience, shared with peers and adults. Qvortrup et al. (1994: 2) argue that 'children are often denied the right to speak for themselves either because they are held incompetent in making judgements or because they are thought of as unreliable witnesses about their own lives'.

Kjørhort (2002: 68–69) views the general movement towards the right of children to participate in decision-making as a 'nodal point' in political and public discourses. However, Kjørhort (2002) believes that the child is constructed in contradictory and paradoxical ways within these discourses. On the one hand children are presented as competent and on a par with adults and on the other hand children are placed in their own world as having their own culture and being under threat from the adults' world.

For Kjørhort (2002) a mythical and nostalgic view of the child in the public narrative is problematic and dangerous as the childhood is presented in an inactive and vulnerable mode. Here the increasing tendency for adults to supervise and organize children's activities within institutions leads to children's culture being threatened in the same way as some animals or plants are endangered.

Sociocultural perspectives of participation

Theoretically, both Rogoff (2003) and Corsaro (2005a) view children's transition into society through the lens of participation in collective mutual communities. What Corsaro et al. (2002) call 'priming events' is similar to Rogoff's notion of 'participatory appropriation' and 'guided participation', while both argue that the personal, interpersonal and institutional should be analysed together, not separately and in isolation. Additionally, they believe that in the process of interpretative reproduction, common and collective activities take place where children construct and produce culture with peers and adults. However, the difference between interpretive reproduction and Rogoff's theory is the fact that the latter does not fully consider the 'the importance of socio-economic and power relations' (Corsaro et al. 2002: 323).

For this reason Corsaro et al. (2002), in their study about children's transition from the preschool to the elementary school in the USA and Italy, focus on the interpersonal, community and individual analysis (as Rogoff 2003), but they extend the process by also looking at peer culture and into the power of social policies in early years education and care which have influenced in the values and activities. Corsaro (2005a) also found that children's participation in adults' initiatives and activities often produces annoyance, confusion, fear and uncertainty due to the power imbalance between the child and the adult. Thus he states that often children's intentions arise as a result of their effort to make sense of the adult's world.

For Corsaro, children's participation in cultural routines is extremely valuable. The daily routines with their vibrancy, predictability, safekeeping and shared understanding provide the habits that make children and adults feel membership of a community, where they can deal with contentious or dubious issues. The process of participation in cultural routines begins from the time that a child is born. It starts as a limited participation based on the 'as-if assumption' (Corsaro 2005a: 19) where the infant is treated as if they are socially competent and goes forward to full participation, not due to the fact that the child learns the rules but due to the security that they feel and control of the activity or the discussion and which the infant then embellishes with new thoughts and activities.

An example of children's participation in telling their own story is given in Case study 7.2.

Case study 7.2: The magic den

Background

The research discussed in this case study is part of an ongoing Outdoor Learning Project (OLP) started in January 2004. The project is based at a state nursery school in England. Children (aged 3 and 4 years) attend the nursery for one year. Visits to a local Country Park are undertaken on one day per week, whatever the weather and here children are supported by practitioners, parents and students. The OLP has evolved a number of 'participatory' methods including the use of video and digital cameras by children to document, reflect on and publish their outdoor experiences (see Waller 2007, 2009).

Field notes and video data recorded by children and researcher April 20th

The children had been on several visits to the Country Park and three children Liam, Charlene and Sammi (pseudonyms), in particular, had played extensively in a wooded copse during their visits. Back at school they discussed with practitioners their desire to make a den. A practitioner had encouraged them to plan out their ideas and helped the children to make a list of tools and equipment they might need to take to the Country Park in order to build the den. Liam appeared to be particularly excited about this prospect and told the key worker that they were going to make a 'Magic Den'. On the next visit to the Country Park, Liam, Charlene and Sammi enlisted the help of a number of other children and they went in search of a location for the den. Having found a location in the woods that they deemed suitable, the children (frequently directed by Liam) started to construct a den that involved placing sticks in the ground and joining them together with string. However, Sammi suggested that they needed a cross-piece to hold the den together. When the children tried to lift the log identified as a cross-piece it was too heavy. A parent offered to lift it up but Liam said 'No we will pull it up with the string'. With some assistance from a practitioner and a parent, a pulley was constructed and the log lifted into place by the children pulling on the string. Charlene then suggested putting a blanket over the top of the den to make it 'like a Magic Den'. Once completed to the children's satisfaction they went inside to play. When it was time to go back to nursery, Charlene said 'I think we will stay here tonight!'

Discussion

Over the course of time, the practitioners and researcher involved in the OLP have endeavoured to evolve a 'participatory' approach to both pedagogy and research. Through exploration and play in the Country Park the children develop themes associated with particular physical objects or spaces – in this case a 'Magic Den'. The children's narratives are supported and co-constructed by other children and adults and confirmed through the publication of pedagogical documentation (Rinaldi 2006). This approach is consistent with Jordan's (2004) model of co-construction where intersubjectivity is developed through adults sharing their own ideas with children to extend their current interests, 'valuing and giving voice to children's activities, respectfully checking that a child would like the offered assistance' (Jordan 2004: 41).

Rogoff (1990) proposed the concept of guided participation to explain the way that children learn as they participate in and, are guided by, the values and practices of their cultural communities. Guided participation involves two basic processes, shared endeavours supported by a mutual structuring of participation (each other's involvement to facilitate engagement in the shared activity) leading to the co-construction of knowledge (Rogoff 2003: 283). In the making of the den it would have been easy for the adults to plan for the children and make the den for the children.

The children's desire to make a 'Magic Den' was constructed during the experience of playing in the woods and reflecting on that experience with other children and skilled practitioners. The den was not planned by adults but it was built through the participation of the adults in supporting the children's desires and competence in their own lives. They experience competence and are recognized as competent (Wenger 1998).

For Rogoff (1997, 2003) 'learning' is a process of improving one's participation in systems of activity, particularly social systems. This is a view that proposes the learner as a social constructor of knowledge through engagement in shared endeavours in cultural communities. Learning and development are therefore inseparable from the concerns of families and interpersonal and community processes. The outdoor learning environments discussed in this case are seen as dynamic and evolving cultural contexts, in which it is meaningless to study the child apart from other people.

Conclusion

This chapter has discussed a number of powerful ideas proposed by the 'new sociology of childhood' and related to the concept of childhood as a social construct. The chapter began with a consideration of how children are identified as 'active in the construction and determination of their own social lives' (James and Prout 1997: 8) and how childhood is viewed as an adult construction that changes over time and place (James and James 2008). Two key concepts, 'agency' and 'participation', were then critically discussed in detail in relation to an ongoing debate about power and the role of adults in the social construction of childhood. In particular the chapter made reference to the sociocultural perspective (Rogoff 2003) and the work of Corsaro to examine the cultural processes of agency and participation. The chapter then discussed recent research by the authors in early years settings to illustrate children's agency and participation in 'telling their own stories'.

The significant contribution of the sociology of childhood to contesting 'normative', singular and static notions of the child and childhood should be recognized. As James (2009) argues, what is most important is for adults to understand children's contribution to society and their right for agency or as Ratner (2000) asserts, the democratic circumstances under which the child can show the potentiality of agency. However, a number of conceptual tensions in these powerful ideas have recently been identified. Uprichard (2008), for example, suggests that the arguments around the child as 'being' and 'becoming' are problematic. She recommends an alternative concept of the child underpinned by the temporality of the two terms. Uprichard (2008) argues that the fact that children are not always children but are moving towards adulthood creates a temporality.

Further, as Bae (2009) and Ratner (2000) contend, there is an overemphasis on the notion of the autonomous child and the other aspect of 'the child in need' is underestimated. Thus Uprichard (2008) and Corsaro (2005b) state that the new sociology of childhood in an effort to define the child as socially constructed individually neglects the great contribution of the development of child through interaction in sociocultural processes. Here, as Smith (2007) states, is the contribution of sociocultural theory; discerning how children are supported in the co-construction of activities (Rogoff 2003). The role of the adult is to sustain and encourage a child's interest to 'help focus on the goal, draw attention to critical features of the task, and reduce the complexity of the task. But there has to be social engagement before children can learn and gradually take on more responsibility' (Smith 2007: 154).

We conclude by arguing that a key challenge in promoting children's participation is how to ensure that children have the space to articulate their views and perspectives beyond the constraints of adult views, interpretation and agenda. There remain reservations about whether children's participation actually results in worthwhile changes and benefits for the children involved (Hill 2006), the danger that participation has become institutionalized and also the possibility that participatory research and practice may actually be exclusionary (Vandenbroeck and Bouverne-De Bie 2006).

In future we need to develop a better conceptual understanding of children's construction of childhood and the significance to children of supporting them to tell their own stories as participants within a learning community. A central problem in this endeavour is that even 'participatory' research with children is part of an adult agenda and that by researching *with* children we may be impacting on their play intentions (Waller and Bitou, forthcoming).

As Waller (2006) argues, we also need to give children space to exercise their agency to participate in their own decisions, actions and meaning making, which may or may not involve them engaging with adults.

Suggested further reading

Corsaro, W.A. (2005) *The Sociology of Childhood*, 2nd edn. Thousand Oaks, CA: Pine Forge Press.
Qvortrup, J., Corsaro, W.A. and Honig, M.S. (eds) (2009) *The Palgrave Handbook of Childhood Studies*. Basingstoke: Palgrave Macmillan.
Rogoff, B. (2003) *The Cultural Nature of Human Development*. Oxford: Oxford University Press.

References

Bae, B. (2009) 'Children's right to participate: Challenges in everyday interactions.' *European Early Childhood Education Research Journal*, 17(3), 391–406.
Cannella, G.S. (1999) 'The scientific discourse of education: Predetermining the lives of others – Foucault, education, and children.' *Contemporary Issues in Early Childhood*, 1(1): 36–44.
Clark, A. and Moss, P. (2001) *Listening to Young Children: The Mosaic approach*. London: National Children's Bureau.
Clark, A. and Moss, P. (2005) *Spaces to Play: More listening to young children using the Mosaic approach*. London: National Children's Bureau.
Corsaro, W.A. (2003) *We're Friends Right? Inside kids' culture*. Washington, DC: Joseph Henry Press.
Corsaro, W.A. (2005a) *The Sociology of Childhood*, 2nd edn. Thousand Oaks, CA: Pine Forge Press.
Corsaro, W.A. (2005b) 'Collective action and agency in young children's peer cultures.' In J. Qvortrup (ed.) *Studies in Modern Childhood: Society, agency, culture*. Basingstoke: Palgrave Macmillan.
Corsaro, W.A. (2009) 'Peer culture.' In J. Qvortrup, W.A. Corsaro and M.S. Honig (eds) *The Palgrave Handbook of Childhood Studies*. Basingstoke: Palgrave Macmillan.
Corsaro, W.A., Molinari, L. and Rosier, B.K. (2002) 'Zena and Carlotta: Transition narratives and early education in the United States and Italy.' *Human Development*, 45: 323–348.
Dahlberg, G., Moss, P. and Pence, A. (2007) *Beyond Quality in Early Childhood Education and Care: Languages of evaluation*, 2nd edn. London: RoutledgeFalmer.
Department of Education and Skills (DfES) (2004a) *Children Act 2004*. London: HMSO.

Department of Education and Skills (DfES) (2004b) *Every Child Matters: Change for Children.* London: HMSO. Available at www.everychildmatters.gov.uk/ (accessed 17 December 2004).

Department for Education and Skills (DfES) (2007) *The Early Years Foundation Stage: Setting the standards for learning, development and care for children from birth to five.* Nottingham: DfES.

Emirbayer, M. and Mische, A. (1998) 'What is agency?' *American Journal of Sociology,* 103(4): 962–1023.

Frønes, I. (2005) 'Structuration of childhood: An essay on the structuring of childhood and anticipatory socialization.' In J. Qvortrup (ed.) *Studies in Modern Childhood: Society, agency, culture.* Basingstoke: Palgrave Macmillan.

Hendrick, H. (1997) 'Constructions and reconstructions of British childhood: An interpretative survey, 1800 to the present.' In A. James and A. Prout (eds) *Constructing and Reconstructing Childhood: Contemporary issues in the sociological study of childhood.* London: RoutledgeFalmer.

Hill, M. (2006) 'Children's voices on ways of having a voice: Children's and young people's perspectives on methods used in research and consultation.' *Childhood,* 13(1): 69–89.

James, A. (2005) 'Life times: Children's perspectives on age, agency and memory across life course.' In J. Qvortrup (ed.) *Studies in Modern Childhood: Society, agency, culture.* Basingstoke: Palgrave Macmillan.

James, A. (2009) 'Agency.' In J. Qvortrup, W.A. Corsaro and M.S. Honig (eds) *The Palgrave Handbook of Childhood Studies.* Basingstoke: Palgrave Macmillan.

James, A. and James, A.L. (eds) (2008) *European Childhoods: Culture, politics and childhood in the European Union.* Basingstoke: Palgrave.

James, A. and Prout, A. (eds) (1997) *Constructing and Reconstructing Childhood: Contemporary issues in the sociological study of childhood,* 2nd edn. London: Falmer.

James, A., Jenks, C. and Prout, A. (1998) *Theorizing Childhood.* Cambridge: Polity.

Jenks, C. (1996) *Childhood.* London: Routledge.

Jordan, B. (2004) 'Scaffolding learning and co-constructing understandings.' In A. Anning, J. Cullen and M. Fleer (eds) *Early Childhood Education.* London: Sage.

Kjørholt, A.T. (2002) 'Small is powerful: Discourses on "Children and Participation" in Norway.' *Childhood,* 9(1): 63–82.

Langsted, O. (1994) 'Looking at quality from the child's perspective.' In P. Moss and A. Pence (eds) *Valuing Quality in Early Childhood Services: New approaches to defining quality.* London: Paul Chapman.

Mayall, B. (2002) *Towards a Sociology of Childhood: Thinking from children's lives.* Buckingham: Open University Press.

Olwig, F. and Gulløv, E. (eds) (2003) *Children's Places: Cross-cultural perspectives.* London: Routledge: Taylor & Francis.

Penn, H. (2005) *Understanding Early Childhood: Issues and controversies.* Maidenhead: Open University Press.

Qvortrup, J. (2009) 'Childhood as a structural form. In J. Qvortrup, W.A. Corsaro and M.S. Honig (eds) *The Palgrave Handbook of Childhood Studies*. Basingstoke: Palgrave Macmillan

Qvortrup, J., Bardy, M., Sgritta, G. and Wintersberger, H. (eds) (1994) *Childhood Matters: Social theory, practice and politics*. Avebury: Aldershot.

Ratner, C. (2000) 'Agency and culture.' *Journal for the Theory of Social Behavior*, 30: 413–434.

Rinaldi, C. (2006) *In Dialogue with Reggio Emilia: Listening, researching and learning*. London: Routledge.

Rogoff, B. (1990) *Apprenticeship in Thinking: Cognitive development in social context*. New York: Oxford University Press.

Rogoff, B. (1997) 'Evaluating development in the process of participation: Theory, methods and practice building on each other.' In E. Amsel and K.A. Renninger (eds) *Change and Development: Issues of theory, method and application*. Mahwah, NJ: Lawrence Erlbaum Associates.

Rogoff, B. (2003) *The Cultural Nature of Human Development*. Oxford: Oxford University Press.

Smith, A.B. (2007) 'Children and young people's participation rights in education.' *International Journal of Children's Rights*, 15: 147–164.

Uprichard, E. (2008) 'Children as "Being and Becomings": Children, childhood and temporality.' *Children and Society*, 22: 303–313.

Vandenbroeck, M. and Bouverne-De Bie, M. (2006) 'Children's agency and educational norms: A tensed negotiation.' *Childhood*, 13(1): 127–143.

Walkerdine, V. (2004) 'Developmental psychology and the study of childhood.' In M.J. Kehily (ed.) *An Introduction to Childhood Studies*. Maidenhead: Open University Press.

Waller, T. (2006) '"Be careful – don't come too close to my Octopus Tree": Recording and evaluating young children's perspectives of outdoor learning.' *Children Youth and Environments*, 16(2): 75–104.

Waller, T. (2007) '"The Trampoline Tree and the Swamp Monster with 18 heads": Outdoor play in the foundation stage and foundation phase.' *Education 3–13*, 35(4): 393–407.

Waller, T. (2009) 'Modern childhood: Contemporary theories and children's lives.' In T. Waller (ed.) *An Introduction to Early Childhood: A multi-disciplinary approach*, 2nd edn. London: Sage.

Waller, T. and Bitou, A. (forthcoming) 'Research with children: Three challenges for participatory research in early childhood.' Submitted to the *European Early Childhood Education Research Association Journal* (accepted November 2009).

Wenger, E. (1998) *Communities of Practice: Learning, meaning and identity*. Cambridge: Cambridge University Press.

8 Applying Bourdieu's concepts of social and cultural capital and habitus to early years research

Jane O'Connor

Pierre-Félix Bourdieu (1930–2002) was one of the best known French sociologists. Born into a postman's family in south western France, he went on to study philosophy in Paris. He worked as a teacher and later as an eminent academic and social theorist. He served in the French army during the Algerian War of Independence during which time he undertook ethnographic research which formed the basis of his sociological reputation. Bourdieu was a prolific writer and researcher and a passionate activist for those he believed subordinated by society. He is held by many to be one of the leading intellectuals of the twentieth century.

This chapter examines the work of Bourdieu (1984, 1989; Bourdieu et al. 1994) and explores how some of his key ideas have been, and can be, applied to research in early childhood. Bourdieu's work is concerned with the central themes of power, class and status, and his writing in education has focused on how such concepts are transmitted in pedagogic contexts, particularly in secondary schools and universities (e.g. Bourdieu et al. 1994). However, although young children do not feature at all in his work, the value of Bourdieu's ideas in understanding social inequalities and differentiated outcomes in the early years is beginning to be recognized. Therefore, throughout this chapter the following question is investigated: 'How has Bourdieu's theoretical approach been used to research and understand how class, status and power are established and reproduced in early years settings?'

The chapter begins with a review of Bourdieu's key concepts and then examines research with young children, their families and early years settings which employ Bourdieu's ideas as a theoretical framework. Implications for practice arising from research findings are then highlighted and the value, and limitations, of Bourdieu's work to the ongoing project of ensuring social justice and cultural equality in early years settings is outlined.

Introduction to Bourdieu's main concepts

Bourdieu conceptualizes the unequal structure of society as being due to a dynamic cause and effect process whereby individuals bring differing amounts of social and cultural 'capital' to the 'game' of life (Grenfell and James 1998). Drawing on classical Marxist theory, Bourdieu expands the concept of economic capital, which relates to the material wealth of individuals and families, to the broader context of the social world. He conceptualizes social life as a game within which there is competition for resources and, according to the rules of the game, those with higher levels of social and cultural capital are more likely to be winners (Gregory et al. 2004). Bourdieu identifies the family as the site of social reproduction and so places great importance on an individual's family background in explaining and predicting their academic performance and life chances in terms of wealth, profession and social status.

Two key terms which Bourdieu uses to define the complex range of influences which families transmit to their children are 'social capital' and 'cultural capital'. In basic terms, social capital refers to *who* you know, whereas cultural capital refers to *what* you know. For example, a newly arrived family in the UK with few, if any, friends in the locality and little or no standing in the community or professionally would be described as being very poor in social capital. In contrast a family who is well established in a local community, who are fluent speakers of the language and who have a strong professional and social standing in the community, perhaps by being school governors or community leaders, would have extremely high levels of social capital. Family structure itself has also been associated with levels of social capital. For example, Coleman (1988), taking a somewhat conservative, anti-feminist stance, claims that social capital is most successfully transmitted in two-parent families where the mother is a full-time housewife, and is most weak in single-parent families.

The related concept of cultural capital refers to the cultural, linguistic and behavioural knowledge and skills which an individual has, which have been learned at home via 'domestic transmission' and which go a long way towards defining who we are in terms of class, culture and social group. Aspects such as one's linguistic ability, knowledge of the dominant culture and knowing how to behave and what to say in various social situations are all part of the cultural capital which is most valued in society. Bourdieu argues that if educationalists do not take account of cultural capital they are liable to perceive 'academic success or failure as an effect of natural aptitudes' rather than take account of 'the best hidden and socially most determinant educational investment, namely, the domestic transmission of cultural capital' (Bourdieu et al. 1994: 47–48). Bourdieu uses this concept of a 'hidden investment' to explain why middle-class children are so often given a head start at school over their counterparts from poorer backgrounds. This is due to the more 'elaborate codes' of speaking which middle-class children tend to learn from their parents, who are more likely to explain the reasons and principles which underlie their reactions to their children's behaviour (Bernstein 1975; Tizard and Hughes 1984), as well as the type of knowledge and experiences which they bring to the setting. Therefore, the power base which determines which people are more likely to be successful in life is uneven right from the start as children start school with hugely different amounts of the 'right' kind of cultural capital. As Brooker (2002: 25) ominously notes: 'Cultural capital requires above all a lengthy period of acquisition, and it is too late to catch up when the child begins statutory schooling'.

It is important to point out here that all children have cultural capital transmitted from their families and cultural context and that, inherently and objectively, no one form of cultural capital is more valuable than any other. However, what Bourdieu highlights is the fact that due to the way in which education systems and professional institutions are structured, some types of cultural capital, namely those forms of knowledge which are traditionally associated with the middle classes, are more valued, and more 'legitimate', than others. Indeed, as Gregory et al. (2004: 88) explain: 'Bourdieu stresses the power of the school as an institution in validating certain forms of "cultural capital" while rejecting others'. Therefore, according to Bourdieu, the amount and type of each capital children have shape their different kinds of knowledge, tastes and ways of thinking and acting which have an impact on each child's potential for being successful in the learning environment. This is not to say, however, that such characteristics, once determined, are fixed throughout life. From Bourdieu's perspective everything is 'up for grabs', everyone is free to play and everything is negotiable (Grenfell and James 1998). Change can be achieved, however, only through a fair and just education system in which every child has the opportunity to fulfil his or her potential as an individual regardless of the social and cultural capital they have 'inherited'.

Another of Bourdieu's key concepts, which is intertwined with the idea of social and cultural capital, is that of 'habitus'. This can be described as an individual's social inheritance or 'unthinking disposition' to act in a certain way, and is, again, acquired in the family and community. The invisible, taken-for-grantedness of one's embodied habitus when an individual is in an environment or 'field' in which they 'fit' is described by Bourdieu (1989: 43) as being 'as a fish in water', with the discomfort of not 'fitting' being the source of potential disassociation and social or educational failure.

Cicourel (1993) describes how habitus can be a useful concept when it comes to exploring: 'how the child acquires a sense of his or her own power and that of adults and peers, as he or she is assigned and assumes different relationships within and outside the family, peer and school settings'

(Cicourel 1993: 109). Bourdieu (1984) explains how 'habitus' is internalized and structured through language and social action and is embodied in individuals through, for example, the way people carry themselves and how they experience and express their thoughts and feelings. Habitus therefore is 'picked up' at home and enacted through the dialectical relationship between an individual's thought and activity and the objective world. It is at once a 'social inheritance' (Robbins 1993) and an unthinking habit or disposition. This disposition has a strong influence on how a child experiences school, and how she/he interacts and engages with the school environment and the people who hold the power therein.

   These concepts of social and cultural capital and habitus can be related to the experiences of very young children as they begin their educational journeys at the age of 4 or 5 or even younger. Indeed, it is in the early edu-care settings where the 'fit' of a child's habitus with the established routines, practices and language of school are first tested and their social and cultural capital is evaluated in relation to peers and practitioners. The following section sets out some illustrative case studies and examines research which has explored these processes in early years settings.

How Bourdieu's work has been applied in the early years

A key aspect of Bourdieu's work which is of critical relevance to young children is in the way that power is structured in early years settings and how children from different families and cultural backgrounds may be disadvantaged or advantaged in this respect. The following case studies of David and Matthew highlight the (mis)fit which can be experienced by young children in early educational settings and raise issues around social and pedagogical practices which can address this, and which are explored later in the chapter.

Case study 8.1: David

David is from Uganda. He is newly arrived in the UK and lives with his father, who is working illegally as a taxi driver. His parents' relationship has broken down and he no longer sees his mother on a regular basis. David and his father know very few people in their new locality and his father's poor English and frequent night work mean that the small family is extremely isolated. David's home is a small, sparsely furnished flat in which there are few toys and no books or educational games. David has not attended any preschool provision in the UK and is entering the Reception class of St Mary's Primary School at age 4.

Case study 8.2: Matthew

Matthew is from a middle-class, affluent family. His parents are well-educated professionals who have socialist leanings and choose to send their children to the local primary school. Matthew's mother is on the board of governors and is much involved with the life of the school from helping to organize cake sales and fun days, to hearing children read and putting up displays. Matthew's older sister, Julia, also attended St Mary's and is now at the local secondary school. Matthew's mother has always read with him, and there are many books and word and number games at home. Matthew attended the nursery which is attached to St Mary's from the age of 3. He knows many of the staff and most of the children in his class already as he moves up into the Reception class at the age of 4.

The two case study examples illustrate the diverse backgrounds of two children starting the same school at age 4 in an economically mixed and culturally diverse area of South London. In terms of social and cultural capital and habitus, it is clear that Matthew has the extreme advantage in this context. Not only does he have the social capital of being part of an influential and established family which is well known to the school, but also he has much cultural capital both in terms of his literacy and numeracy knowledge and in terms of his understanding of how the school environment works and what is expected of him here. David, on the other hand, can be described as being poor not only in social and cultural capital, but also in economic terms. He and his father are unknown in the area and have no connections to the school or to other children and families. David has had many experiences in his short life and has much knowledge about his home country, yet this will not translate into cultural capital at his new school. He knows little of books and has few shared cultural experiences in common with his teacher and peers. Additionally his English is poor compared to Matthew's fluent language and wide vocabulary. David's 'habitus' renders him completely unfamiliar to the school setting, whereas Matthew's habitus makes his entry into school seamless.

    This issue of the social and cultural inequality of children starting school was researched by Brooker (2002), who undertook an ethnographic investigation into class, culture and pedagogy in young children's learning. In her study Brooker focused on a group of 4-year-old working-class children and their families as they started school in urban Britain in the late 1990s. She explored issues around how the home experience of children from poor and ethnic minority communities influenced their adaptation to school and questioned the extent to which the pedagogies of early years classrooms met the needs of children from culturally diverse backgrounds. Drawing on Bourdieu's concepts of cultural and social capital and habitus, Brooker (2002) explains how some children are set up to fail from the outset due to the unfamiliarity of the school environment in terms of language, practices and values. Brooker describes how the children's home life and parental attitudes, beliefs and traditions, if not fully integrated into the pedagogic and social practices of the setting, can disadvantage a child and lead to a failure to learn.

From her research with the children and their families, Brooker (2002) identified three key aspects of cultural capital which seem to be most predictive of children's school achievements. These are mothers' educational experiences, family language and communicative skills, and family literacy practices (Brooker 2002: 33). A lack of capital in these areas was found to be exacerbated in families where the home language was not English. This was because of the inherent difficulties of parents not being able to support their child's learning in English when it is not their first language, and also because of the barrier of being unfamiliar with the routines and structure of the educational system which they may not have attended and in which their child was now participating.

In relation to social capital Brooker (2002) found that although it was low in many of the families studied, there was an internal hierarchy whereby some families were more highly ranked than others and had easier access to the influential institution of the school. In Brooker's study, these families tended to be Anglo, with Bangladeshi families having forms of social capital which were less likely to be effective in the field of education. Reay (1998) has researched the related issue of the lack of communication which can occur between teachers and families who possess different kinds of cultural and social capital than that recognized as valuable by the school. In her research Reay (1998) notes the easy access to school and teachers enjoyed by more affluent and/or more highly educated parents, which is also noted by Brooker (2002).

Brooker (2002) investigated the concept of habitus in exploring the social and educational inequalities which her study uncovered. She explains habitus as being unique to each child as well as each family, and interprets it as a set of dispositions, acquired through the home, which influence rather than determine a child's behaviour. For example, patterns of adaptation through the first few days of school can be vastly different for children from different families and this transition is much smoother for those children whose home cultures and values reflect those of the school more closely. As Brooker notes: 'How families choose to invest and exploit their various forms of capital counts equally for their children who in their earliest years are learning ways of behaving which they will take with them into the classroom' (Brooker 2002: 42).

Brooker highlights the role of the school in minimizing the educational inequalities which arise from differences in capital and habitus among young children. She criticizes not individual practitioners who generally have the best of intentions towards nurturing the potential of all the children in their class, but the way in which early years settings are often based on an 'exclusive western view of childhood, and a specifically western way of learning, which for some children creates a barrier to learning in the classroom' (Brooker 2002: 163). (See Waller and Bitou, Chapter 7 in this volume, for further discussion of the western view of childhood.) Brooker encourages practitioners to challenge their 'taken for granted' beliefs around learning and calls for a more diverse perspective to be taken to early years education and the development of a more central role for parents and families in school from the very beginning.

Lareau (2000, 2003) has also undertaken ethnographic research to explore issues of educational inequality using the work of Bourdieu as a theoretical framework. She is particularly interested in the processes by which families and individuals come to understand their roles in the social class system and the key role which the socialization of young children can have in perpetuating the cycle of disadvantage. However, it is important to be aware that it is not only among teachers and parents that issues of capital and habitus become translated into significant social processes. Children themselves can reproduce stereotypical and differentiated ways of being through their interactions with each other from a very early age. Research has been undertaken which focuses on the agency of children in reproducing inequality drawing on the 'new' sociology of childhood (James and Prout 1997) which emphasizes the active role children play in social life. For example, Reay (1995) has explored how the concept of habitus can be used to analyse peer group interaction and explore how differences of gender, 'race' and class are produced by children in primary classrooms. She notes how the children in her study created a hierarchy in the classroom via subtle processes of marginalization through voice, language, gesture and attitude. 'Children are not innocent of cultural re/production', Reay (1995: 368) claims, 'They are not simply products of their parents'.

The extent to which these processes may occur in early years settings has yet to be explored, but it is important to acknowledge the active role children take in their own socialization and to note that a high proportion of communication and interaction in a classroom is not adult led. What does seem clear is the way in which children's habitus impacts on their experience of school both in terms of the formal and the informal curriculum.

Gregory et al. (2004) further explore the symbolic forms of capital which different children bring to the early years setting in their study of introducing literacy to 4 year olds. They outline how classroom culture and teacher–child interactions can maximize learning opportunities and potential for all children. Taking as their starting point the principal aim of the National Curriculum, which is 'to ensure equality of opportunity for all children, regardless of race or social class' (Gregory et al. 2004: 85), they question whether children living in very different economic circumstances are really given equal access to literacy during their first year at school. Their ethnographic study aimed to explore the variation in attainment by children of different backgrounds in literacy. They did this by documenting what 'actually takes place between teachers and children during day-to-day interaction' (Gregory et al. 2004: 86) in three schools which varied greatly in terms of the socio-economic characteristics of the catchment area and the ethnic composition of the school populations. Through their study they examined the 'microculture' of the early years classrooms in these schools, and analysed how pupil–teacher interactions can differ in different communities, and most crucially, which types of discourse tend to lead to early school literacy success.

Gregory et al. (2004) found that the schools differed in many aspects, including their approaches to teaching and learning, the type of questioning they employed with the children, the value they put on working 'hard', the celebration of children's work and praise for their achievements, and their attitudes towards parents being included in the school environment. Overall it was evident that in the more middle-class, affluent school, parents were more readily welcomed into the classroom. Furthermore, their children enjoyed a comfortable adaptation to school literacy lessons as they started school with a knowledge of literary lexicon such as 'sentence' and 'spelling' and were already familiar with many of the stories and texts which were used at school to teach reading. Additionally, the children in the middle-class school were encouraged to bring in cultural artefacts from home and share them with the class, which supported their ability to make frequent connections between what they were learning in-school and what they already knew. Indeed, from the very first lesson, Gregory et al. (2004: 93) describe how children in this school were already saying 'I knew that'. This sharing of home and school knowledge advantaged the children in their literacy skills both explicitly in terms of what they knew about reading, books, spelling and so on, and implicitly in terms of valuing the kinds of things they knew – their literacy 'capital' as it were. In contrast, in the other school, communication problems often arose when the teacher 'implicitly assumed that the children could...draw upon a bank of *shared cultural knowledge* with herself from their homes or had shared linguistic expectations in relation to school tasks' (Gregory et al. 2004: 100).

However, Gregory et al. (2004) emphasize that the affluence and social class of the school population does not have to determine children's success in the early years setting and that careful pedagogic strategies can overcome such inequity. For example, they describe how one teacher in the study created 'a particular culture within her class that defies existing paradigms of social class, capital and early school success' (Gregory et al. 2004: 85). This teacher ensured that she shared and respected a similar interpretation of 'work' and trying hard with the children's parents, thereby reinforcing the children's feelings of success and belonging in the school environment. She also did not expect the children to have knowledge of British culture or language, and did not call upon their social, economic or cultural resources in her teaching, which was based on a visible explicit pedagogy and the use of instructional discourse. Interestingly Gregory et al. (2004) reported that the children from the middle-class school were no further ahead in literacy at the end of their first year at school than those at the school just described, many of whom lived in short-term hostels with families who had little in terms of economic, social and cultural resources.

All these ethnographic studies have in common the aim to 'call into question the self-evident' (Alasuutari 1995: 145) and this methodological approach fits well with Bourdieu's aim to critique the seemingly accepted and increasingly naturalized disparity between the educational achievements of children from rich and poor families.

In their study of early years settings in France, Chamboredon and Prévot (2004: 349) conclude that the nursery school is 'an institution and a market where the habits produced by the family are moulded, developed and standardized'. In the UK, it seems, the habits produced by the family are just as likely to be disregarded as to be moulded and developed in an early years setting. It is this issue that generates important implications of Bourdieu's analysis for professional practice, and these are explored below.

Implications for professional practice

There is growing focus in the UK on the benefits of integrated services for children, families and communities using a social capital framework. For example, Sure Start children's centres were trialled and set up by the UK government in the late 1990s and early 2000s in an attempt to redress the unequal 'starting point' of children from disadvantaged areas when they begin school compared to their more affluent counterparts (DCSF 2009). The idea behind these children's centres is that they are a 'one-stop shop' which meet the needs of children and families in terms of education, care, health and social services all under one roof in the most deprived areas of the UK. Ironically, the reality is that such centres are now often utilized more by middle-class mothers who are keen to access high quality services for their children, than those from more disadvantaged backgrounds whom they were intended to benefit (Bennett 2006). Indeed research indicates that poorer families may be mistrustful of any form of perceived state interventions in their child-rearing activities or may feel nervous about engaging with children's services at all (Jones et al. 2008). From a Bourdieuan perspective then, this is a clear example of high levels of social capital rendering middle-class mothers more comfortable accessing professional support and guidance and having the confidence to take what they need and want from the services available to them. Another winning strategy in the 'game of life'.

Subsequently, the challenge remains for practitioners to ensure that all children entering their settings are given equal opportunities to succeed educationally whatever their cultural, economic or social capital may be. This is no easy task given the myriad unintentional, subtle ways in which processes of including and valuing some, and excluding others, occurs in the course of everyday life and interactions in all educational environments. However, the importance of meeting this challenge is of utmost importance in early years settings as it is generally here that the child engages with the wider world of institutionalized power for the first time.

As Comber (1999) notes in her study of US children's readiness for learning when they start school, what counts and is valued as knowledge may be very different for different children. She highlights that it is a skilled practitioner who is able to appreciate the kinds of knowledge, experience and social and cultural capital that children bring with them into school. She explains how:

> Sometimes teachers discount children's preschool, home and community experiences as limited, non-existent or chaotic. Teachers need to learn about how children live in homes and communities – the complexity of networks that support families with minimal economic resources, their sophisticated multilingual and/or multi-modal language use and production, their multiple responsibilities for siblings and elders, the independent negotiation of service encounters, their encyclopaedic knowledge of television and popular culture.
>
> (Comber 1999: 6)

In this sense it is the teachers, perhaps even more so than the children, who need to be 'ready' for learning and this seems to be the central implication for practice which can be learnt from applying Bourdieu's ideas to the early years.

From the research reviewed in this chapter then, the following implications for practice seem key:

- Practitioners need to be aware of the various forms of cultural capital which children 'bring' with them to school in terms of linguistic and cultural knowledge and place equal value on these.
- Communication with parents is of paramount importance. Settings need to ensure all parents have the opportunity to be involved in the life of the school and that routines and pedagogic practices are fully transparent and understood by all.
- Children's interactions with each other need to be monitored and children need to be given guidance and support in accepting and embracing the differences between them rather than forming 'cliques' based on similarities in terms of social and cultural capital.

- Criteria of success in settings should not be dependent on children being familiar with British culture or language and should not disadvantage children who have different dispositions or 'habitus'.
- Children's home life and parental attitudes, beliefs and traditions should be fully integrated into the pedagogic and social practices of the setting through home–school links, multilingual learning resources and recognition and celebration of the cultures and languages reflected in the classroom.

It is encouraging to note that the Early Years Foundation Stage Framework (DCSF 2008), which was rolled out in England in 2008 for all children aged 0 to 5 embraces some of these principles in theory and practice. For example, in relation to providing for equality of opportunity the framework states that: 'Providers have a responsibility to ensure positive attitudes to diversity and difference – not only so that every child is included and not disadvantaged, but also so that they learn from the earliest age to value diversity in others.'

A further aim relates to ensuring strong links with parents and families:

> Close working between early years' practitioners and parents is vital for the identification of children's learning needs ... Parents and families are central to a child's well-being and practitioners should support this important relationship by sharing information and offering support for extending learning in the home.
>
> (DCSF 2008: 10)

It is also reassuring that the early learning goals include helping children to 'understand that people have different needs, views and cultures and beliefs that need to be treated with respect'.

The extent to which the EYFS Framework will be effective in balancing out educational outcomes for all children remains to be seen, but in principle issues of cultural and social diversity and equality are clearly central to its philosophy.

This chapter has outlined Bourdieu's powerful ideas about the social and cultural transmission of inequality and reviewed research which has explored these themes as they relate to the earliest years of a child's education. It has made recommendations for practice based on the findings of these studies and has indicated how current educational policy for the early years in England is addressing issues of social and cultural inclusion and equity which have been expounded by Bourdieu for many years. However, although Bourdieu's work has been demonstrated as being of value in explaining issues of power and diversity in early years settings, it is also important to acknowledge the limitations of a theory which is based on empirical research solely in France. Furthermore, Bourdieu's theories have been criticized for placing too much emphasis on the internalization of feelings of inferiority within individuals who are not of the dominant class in educational settings, and failing to fully recognize the external barriers to exclusion which are arguably at least as great as any internal sense of cultural unworthiness (Kennett 1973). Feminists have also drawn attention to the neglect of issues of gender in much of Bourdieu's writings (McLeod 2005).

Nevertheless, at the heart of Bourdieu's work is the key acknowledgement that it is the routines of everyday life which serve to maintain and reproduce inequality. It is these routines and 'taken for granted' practices which need to be constantly critically examined and reflected upon if we are to ensure early years' settings serve to minimize educational inequality rather than magnify it.

Suggested further reading

Ball, S. (2002) *Class Strategies and the Education Market: The middle classes and social advantage*. London: Routledge.
Grenfell, M. (2008) *Pierre Bourdieu: Key concepts*. Durham: Acumen.
Jenkins, R. (2002) *Pierre Bourdieu*. London: Routledge.

References

Alasuutari, P. (1995) *Researching Culture: Qualitative method and cultural studies*. London: Sage.
Bennett, R. (2006) 'Poor turned off Sure Start by middle-class mothers.' *Timesonline*. Available at www.timesonline.co.uk/tol/news/uk/article663212.ece (accessed 13 April 2010).
Bernstein, B. (1975) *Class, Codes and Control*. London: Routledge & Kegan Paul.
Bourdieu, P. (1984) *Distinction: A social critique of the judgement of taste*. Cambridge, MA: Harvard University Press.
Bourdieu, P. (1989) In L. Wacquant, 'Towards a reflexive sociology: A workshop with Pierre Bourdieu.' *Sociological Theory*, 7: 26–63.
Bourdieu, P., Passeron, J.C. and de Saint Martin, M. (1994) *Academic Discourse*. Cambridge: Polity.
Brooker, L. (2002) *Starting School: Young children learning cultures*. Buckingham: Open University Press.
Chamboredon, J. and Prévot, J. (2004) 'Changes in the social definition of early childhood and the new forms of symbolic violence.' *Theory and Society*, 2(1): 331–350.
Cicourel, A.V. (1993) 'Aspects of structural and processual theories of knowledge.' In C. Calhoun, E. Lipuma and M. Postune (eds) *Bourdieu: Critical perspectives*. Cambridge: Polity.

Coleman, J. (1988) 'Social capital in the creation of human capital.' *American Journal of Sociology*, 94(suppl.): S95–S120.

Comber, B. (1999) '"Coming, ready or not!": What counts as early literacy?' *Language and Literacy*, 1. Available at www.langandlit.ualberta.ca/archives/vol11papers/coming.htm (accessed 21 October 2009).

DCSF (2008) *Early Years Foundation Stage Framework*. Available at www://nationalstrategies.standards.dcsf.gov.uk (accessed 4 March 2010).

DCSF (2009) *Sure Start Children's Centres*. Available at www.dcsf.gov.uk/everychildmatters/earlyyears/surestart/whatsurestartdoes/ (accessed 9 November 2009).

Gregory, E., Williams, A., Baker, D. and Street, B. (2004) 'Introducing literacy to four year olds: Creating classroom cultures in three schools.' *Journal of Early Childhood Literacy*, 4: 85–107.

Grenfell, M. and James, D. (1998) *Bourdieu and Education*. London: Falmer.

James, A. and Prout, A. (1997) *Constructing and Reconstructing Childhood*. London: Routledge.

Jones, P., Moss, D., Tomlinson, P. and Welch, S. (2008) *Childhood: Services and provision for children*. Harlow: Pearson.

Kennett, J. (1973) 'The sociology of Pierre Bourdieu.' *Educational Review*, 25(3): 237–249.

Lareau, A. (2000) *Home Advantage: Social class and parental intervention in elementary education*. Lanham, MD: Rowman & Littlefield.

Lareau, A. (2003) *Unequal Childhoods: Class, race and family life*. Berkeley, CA: University of California Press.

McLeod, J. (2005) 'Feminists re-reading Bourdieu.' *Theory and Research in Education*, 3(1): 11–30.

Reay, D. (1995) '"They employ cleaners to do that": Habitus in the primary classroom.' *British Journal of Sociology of Education*, 16(3): 353–371.

Reay, D. (1998) *Class Work: Mothers' involvement in their children's schooling*. London: UCL Press.

Robbins, A. (1993) 'The practical importance of Bourdieu's analyses of higher education.' *Studies in Higher Education*, 18(2): 151–63.

Tizard, B. and Hughes, M. (1984) *Young Children Learning, Talking and Thinking at Home and at School*. London: Fontana.

9 Freire revisited: critical literacy – whose story is it anyway?

Rohan Jowallah

Introduction

Paulo Freire (1921–1997) is one of the most prominent educational scholars of the late twentieth century. Born in Brazil, Freire had a brief career in law before making a career change to education. Although Freire came from a 'middle-class' family background, he became very interested in the education of the less privileged in Brazil. Freire viewed literacy as a tool for empowerment from the oppressed. Based on his educational ideologies, he was arrested twice in his home country. Although Freire died in 1997, his work continues to be of high relevance to educators, policymakers and academics.

This chapter offers an overview of the key concepts of critical literacy pedagogy from a Freirean prespective; it highlights critical literacy in practice in early years settings using case studies and critically evaluates the appropriateness of using critical literacy in early years settings. This chapter links case studies from my research and recent publications to offer a guide to how critical literacy can be implemented in practice to enhance children's voices in early childhood. This includes demonstrating how the practitioner can utilize a number of strategies that could engage a child and guide the child's thinking. These strategies could include 'gender switch', 'theme switch', 'setting switch', 'clothing switch', 'emotion switch', 'ethnic/race switch' or 'language switch' according to McLaughlin and DeVoogd (2004a). The chapter also discusses how critical literacy, although beneficial for children in the early years, can also be problematic; it considers potential tensions within practice and how the practitioner could mediate these. Although the EYFS age range is from 0 to 5 years, this chapter focuses on children from age 5 and older. I believe that children aged 5 and older are able to begin to engage more in critical issues based on their wider experiences of the world and literacy and their emotional development of engaging with texts.

Becoming literate

Finding a specific definition for literacy is complicated based on the perspectives that individuals may have of literacy. For example, one early years teacher could define literacy as the skills children need to gain competencies in reading. However, another early years teacher could define literacy as the tools children need to read and understand the world around them. For Freire literacy was more than acquiring specific skills. Freire (1993) emphasized that being literate meant being able to read, write and engage in social issues. Freire also suggests that reading cannot be neutral, based on the social and political context in which literacy takes place. In other words, there is always an intention behind texts or discourses and these intentions are important in understanding objectives of writers or talkers. For example, in the nursery rhyme 'London Bridge is falling down' the story behind this rhyme is rarely explored. As a child, I sang this rhyme in Jamaica without having knowledge of the historical issues within the content of the rhyme (the Great Fire of London in 1666). It is essential to get children thinking about the meaning of texts at an early age as this could over time develop their understanding that texts could contain hidden messages.

If literacy is viewed as acquisition of specific skills, the concept of literacy will be reduced. I believe that Freire's (1993) concerns regarding this reductionist approach are still valid, based on the emphasis being placed on literacy targets by our policymakers. This reductionist approach, according to Freire, can also lead to illiteracy. Freire (2005) affirms that being illiterate

> is a handicap to the extent that in literate cultures it interdicts illiterates by preventing them from completing the cycle in the relationship between language, thought and reality and by closing the doors to writing, which represents an important and necessary means of understanding relationships.
>
> (Freire 2005: 3)

For Freire (2005), the relationship between language, thought and reality is important, as it helps to form an understanding of the social world. If children are taught consistently to perform to meet specific targets in literacy, this will limit their understanding of social issues. Like Freire, the writer believes it is essential that literacy is connected to the social context in which it takes place. It is therefore important to provide children with the appropriate opportunities for literacy exchange to increase their understanding of the world. Gee (1990: 27) suggests that literacy can take place within different social contexts. He states there are 'multiple ways in which reading, writing and language interrelate with the workings of power and desire in social life'. Therefore, consideration should be given to the sociocultural theories on literacy, which place emphasis on 'literacy events, literacy practices and performances' (Kucer 2005: 197).

Critical literacy

According to Stribling (2008: 4), Freire 'stressed the importance of critically examining the world in which we live and work in order to name existing inequities and begin to transform oppressive structures through the power of words (spoken, read, and written)'. While there is no single academic definition of critical literacy, it can be viewed as an approach that requires participants to examine texts, conversations and media using a critical perspective. Critical literacy invites readers to actively analyse texts while offering different perspectives of viewing the text. Within definitions for critical literacy there are dominant themes which suggest that critical literacy is social, political and cultural practices employed in the reading, writing and communication process in relation to different forms of media; it involves power relations, identification of ideologies within text, highlighting issues of inequality and injustice and critical reflection on one's position in relation to text (Freire 1970; Kretovics 1985; Bizzell and Herzberg 1996; Morgan 1997). Importantly, Vasquez (2004: 3) suggests: 'Critical literacy does not necessarily involve a negative stance; rather it means looking at an issue or topic in different ways, analysing it, and hopefully being able to suggest possibilities for change or improvement'.

The concept of engaging children in early years in critical literacy may seem challenging. However, I believe that during childhood children are formulating their own perceptions of the world. Therefore, critical engagement is needed to challenge possible views: these views if left unchallenged could lead to the isolation of specific groups within our society and the development of oppressive ideologies. For example, a teacher could plan a critical literacy session in response to negative comments made by children in relation to a specific group within our society. This engagement would challenge children's perspectives and give children alternative perspectives. However, if the teacher fails to engage, this could lead to the affirmation of these oppressive ideologies.

Principles of critical literacy pedagogy

Freire wanted a system of education that would meet the needs of individuals in Brazil and allow individuals to develop their own character. Before Freire's movement, other individuals tried to develop similar schools of thought. According to Hannon (2007: 23), 'In the nineteenth-century Britain for example, working class political aspirations included a concern with literacy and universal suffrage'. Hannon (2007: 23) uses the example of William Lovell, who 'in 1841 made a detailed proposal for a method of teaching reading and writing ... to replace learning by rote'. For Hannon (2007: 23), Lovett wanted a method that 'enables the oppressed to understand what was being done to them'. Hannon (2007: 23) argues that, 'Only in modern times have the least powerful been expected to acquire literacy and then the kind of literacy thought appropriate for them may differ from that exercised by the powerful'. Both Freire's and Lovett's desire for literacy coincide, even though they were years apart, and can be linked to new studies in literacy development. Both individuals appear to subscribe to the view that literacy has a social function.

Freire's pedagogy of literacy has been established on a number of key beliefs. According to Freire (1973: 37), 'the first stage must deal with the problem of the oppressed consciousness and the oppressor consciousness'. This links directly to the views of Freire and Macedo (1987: 29) that 'Reading does not consist merely of decoding the words and language; rather, it is preceded by and intertwined with knowledge of the world'. For Freire, literacy is primarily concerned with the relationship between ideology and political consciousness' (Larson and Marsh 2005: 41). The second tenet of Freire's pedagogy is dialogue. For Freire (1973: 47), dialogue is 'Critical and liberating ... which presupposes action'. This dialogue should be inclusive with all the partners involved (teacher and children). As Larson and Marsh (2005: 41) contend, 'children and teachers are partners in the learning process rather than participating in hierarchical models of power'. Freire's third tenet was based on the need for prior knowledge. According to Freire (1973: 49), 'the oppressed engage in reflection on their concrete situation ... reflection – true reflection – leads to action'. Aronowitz (1993) states that:

> Freire emphasizes 'reflection', in which the student assimilates knowledge in accordance with his/her own needs rather than rote learning and is dedicated, like some elements of the progressive tradition to helping the learner become a subject of his/her own education rather an object of the system's education agenda.
>
> (Aronowitz 1993: 9)

Freire believed that educators should avoid banking models of education and outlines some of the features of these banking models as follows:

> The teacher teaches and the children are taught; the teacher knows everything and the children know nothing; the teacher talks and the children listen – meekly; and the teacher is the subject of the learning process while the pupils are mere objects.
>
> (Freire 1973: 52)

The 'banking model' outlined by Freire suggests that teachers are seen as the main facilitators of knowledge. In this situation children's experiences are not utilized, as the teacher is seen as the main source of knowledge. For Freire, this model leads to oppression based on the method employed by the educators.

Freire's tenets for critical literacy form common ground with McLaughlin and DeVoogd's (2004b: 15) tenets for critical literacy. First, McLaughlin and DeVoogd (2004b: 14) believe 'Critical Literacy focuses on issues of power and promotes reflection, transformation, and action'. Second, 'Critical literacy focuses on the problem and its complexity'. Third, 'Critical literacy strategies are dynamic and adapt to the contexts in which they are used'. Fourth, 'literacy disrupts the commonplace by examining issues from multiple perspectives' (McLaughlin and DeVoogd 2004b: 14).

The first tenet outlined by McLaughlin and DeVoogd (2004b: 14) suggests that 'we as readers may use our power to question the perspective and engage in reflection about whose voice might be missing, discounted, or silenced'. Based on the reflection, alternative views are given; these alternative views, according to McLaughlin and DeVoogd (2004b), will lead to 'transformation'. Therefore, literacy educators need to examine the design of text and production of text, thus providing a medium for evaluation leading to transformation (Janks 2000; Vasquez 2001). According to Stribling (2008: 36), texts can be used as a 'springboard' to explore issues of 'social injustices'. Within these explorations, children and teachers, 'politicise themselves and engage in action challenging existing structures of inequality and oppression' (Cummins and Sayer 1995: 23). McLaughlin and DeVoogd (2004b: 14) warn 'Good intentions or awareness of an unjust situation will not transform it. We must act on our knowledge'. The need for action is essential for this aspect of critical literacy; therefore, it is necessary to 'adopt practices that will not only open up new possibilities but also will begin to deal with taking action' (O'Brien 2001: 53).

The second tenet outlined by McLaughlin and DeVoogd (2004b: 15) suggests 'Critical literacy focuses on the problem and its complexity'. According to McLaughlin and DeVoogd (2004b: 15), 'In critical literacy, rather than accepting an essentialist view, we would engage in problematizing – seeking to understand the problem and its complexity'. McLaughlin and DeVoogd (2004b) also suggest this approach would involve the seeking of an 'alternative explanation' in order to gain additional comprehension of the situation. Lankshear (1997) also supports this perspective outlined by McLaughlin and DeVoogd (2004b) and postulates that critical literacy includes critical views in relation to language and literacy (Lankshear 1997); this also takes into account the wider social context.

The third dominant tenet outlined by McLaughlin and DeVoogd (2004b) is the fact that 'critical literacy strategies are dynamic and adapt to the context in which they are used'. McLaughlin and DeVoogd (2004b: 15) believe: 'There is not a list of methods in critical literacy that work the same in all contexts at the same time. No technique that promotes critical literacy can be exported to another setting without adapting it'.

This view is reiterated by Freire (2005: xi), who states: 'It is impossible to export pedagogical practices without reinventing them'. Therefore, teachers of critical literacy will need to make their own adjustments before implementing critical literacy into their setting (Meacham 2003).

Luke and Freebody (1999) suggest that, for active participation within classroom, children will need to be actively involved in code breaking of text (understanding the hidden messages in text). McLaughlin and DeVoogd (2004b: 16) state: 'readers need to understand that they have the power to envision alternative ways of viewing the author's topic, and they exert that power, when they read from a critical stance'. McLaughlin and DeVoogd (2004b) urge teachers of critical literacy to ensure that the feedback given by children is consistent with the principles of critical literacy. Therefore, these responses should not seek to oppress or delimit other social groups or individuals. For example, a child could respond negatively to a particular individual during a discussion. The teacher on hearing these comments should respond appropriately by telling the child his or her response was inappropriate.

The final tenet outlined by McLaughlin and DeVoogd (2004b) is 'Critical literacy disrupts the commonplace by examining it from multiple perspectives'. By using multiple perspectives, this may 'challenge children to expand their thinking and discover diverse beliefs, position and understanding' (McLaughlin 2001: 15). Adapting a multiple perspective, children could develop 'critical stance' of the issue under investigation (Lewison et al. 2002; see also McLaughlin 2001). For example, children could be shown a picture and asked to suggest two reasons why this picture was taken. This simple task could yield many perspectives which could be used for further discussion. The same task could also be extended to a piece of writing for older children.

Jowallah (2010) suggests that there are seven essential features for the implementation and evaluation of critical literacy: 'validation of critical literacy', 'motivation and participation', 'children's voices', 'social justice and equality', 'environment', 'transformation through reflection' and 'power dynamic'.

Validation of critical literacy

Individuals who are involved in critical literacy should be aware that literacy goes beyond the skills of decoding of words. Those who engage in critical literacy should understand that critical literacy is reading the word, as well as the world (Freire 1973). In addition, the teaching of literacy should be viewed as a social and political practice (Freire 1993: 115). For the 'validation of critical literacy', early years practitioners would need to conceptualize literacy as a social practice linked to children's social and cultural background. By viewing critical literacy as social practice, practitioners could link children's communication, speaking and writing within the social and cultural experiences of the children. Freire (1973) highlighted the importance of reading the 'world' and the 'word'.

Motivation and participation

Critical literacy pedagogy takes into consideration dominant discourses within the society and culture. Sections of these discourses should ensure that children are motivated to participate. Both the teacher and children are partners in the learning process (Grambrell et al. 1996; McLaughlin and DeVoogd 2004b). One way in which practitioners in early years could motivate and improve children's participation is to make connection to children's popular culture. According to Larson and Marsh (2005: 114), 'Children are immersed in a world in which popular culture is linked to a growing number of leisure pursuits'. Therefore, engagement of children in popular culture could lead to increased motivation and participation for children and be linked to the school's literacy practices in a purposeful way (Pompe 1996; Dyson 1998; Marsh 1999).

Children's voices

Within a critical literacy framework, children should be able to contribute to the curriculum. This level of engagement will be essential for children's motivation and engagement. Children could develop their voice (agency) by engaging in conversations (see Chapter 7). Practitioners can use conversation to initiate and develop thinking skills. Children's voices could also enhance child-led learning within the context of the Early Years Foundation Stage (DfES 2007) as children may develop more confidence in sharing ideas with their peers.

Social justice and equality

Critical literacy pedagogy seeks to highlight issues of social injustices in order to promote equality, empowerment and critical thinking in individuals. The concept of social justice could be somewhat difficult to perceive within the context of children in early years. However, if children are allowed to engage in discourse linked to social justice and equality within our society then this could be a step forward in understanding social issues within the world. The issue of social justice and equality could be explored when practitioners focus on children's personal, social and emotional development within the context of the EYFS. For example, the EYFS highlights the need for children to develop a respect for their own culture and beliefs and those of others.

Environment

Children and teachers should work towards the creation of a safe and secure environment in which critical literacy can take place. There should be an atmosphere of trust where children can express their views. A critical literacy environment cannot be exported, but needs to be conceptualized by those involved within the class environment (Freire 2005). Within an early years environment, practitioners could also consider ways in which they could also enhance the creativity and critical thinking of children.

Transformation through reflection

Engagement within a critical literacy framework will require teachers to have dedication and an ideological framework for the transformation to social equality. Children should be guided by the teacher for this level of transformation and reflection to take place (Janks 2000; Vasquez 2001).

Power dynamic

Critical literacy is dynamic and will at times lead to a shift of power from teacher to children. Therefore, understanding the power dynamics within discourse is essential for the success of critical literacy (Beck 2005). Within the context of early years this should not be a potential barrier as children are engaged in many activities in which they take the lead in their own learning.

From my own research, I would like to propose a framework (Figure 9.1) for the implementation and assessment of critical literacy: 'understanding the seven features of critical literacy' (Stage 1), 'assessment of readiness for critical literacy' (Stage 2), 'planning and negotiation' (Stage 3), 'critical literacy in action' (Stage 4) and 'assessment of critical literacy in action' (Stage 5). The first stage of the framework (Figure 9.1) outlines the need for teachers to understand the features of critical literacy. Once teachers have gained knowledge of these seven features, an assessment could be undertaken to evaluate children's readiness to engage in critical literacy (Stage 2). By doing the assessment, teachers could explore children's attitudes towards critical literacy, children's shared interests along with social and cultural issues that could impact on critical literacy. After the assessment of readiness for critical literacy, the teacher and children would engage in the planning of the learning activities (Stage 3).

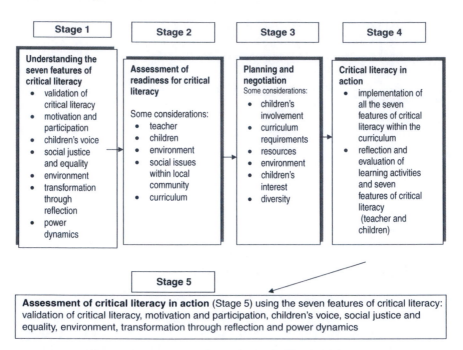

Figure 9.1 A framework for the implementation and assessment of critical literacy.

Planning will also require the teacher and children to have negotiations within the context of the curriculum requirements and the seven features of critical literacy. After the planning and negotiation of critical literacy, activities discussed would be put into practice (Stage 4). It will also be essential for the teacher to evaluate the lessons taught using critical literacy in relation to the seven features outlined in Stage 1.

The work by Vasquez (2004) highlights how critical literacy was implemented within an early years curriculum. The case study outlines Vasquez's clear understanding of critical literacy. In addition, the case illustrates children's readiness to engage in critical literacy and children and teacher working two the planning of activities.

Case study 9.1: The school barbecue

As Vasquez (2004) outlines, children as young as 4 years old can be involved in critical literacy when social connections are made.

The social issue evolved from a barbecue held at the school. In this situation, consideration had not been given to Anthony, a vegetarian, who attended the school barbecue. Consequently, Anthony was unable to partake of the food.

According to Vasquez (2004: 104), 'The children were upset that no one had thought about having food for vegetarians at the barbecue and that no one had asked if there were vegetarians in our school'. Using the concerns of children, Vasquez scaffolded children into the examination of the flyers (advertisement) used to promote the barbecue. The first line of the advertisement read: 'Join us for our Annual School Barbecue' (Vasquez 2004: 104). The use of the pronoun 'us' suggested that the barbecue was for everyone. However, as children discussed the pronoun (us), they stated the barbecue was not for Anthony (vegetarian) because there was no provision for him. This discussion led to how pronouns work to position the reading in relation to the reading material. In this situation, children decided to write a letter to the school's administrator. During the draft, children selected the best words to use.

Vasquez (2004) and her children did extended work relating to critical literacy and highlights how critical literacy can be implemented within an early years setting.

In her work, Vasquez uses children's interest to motivate them in the literacy process. In one situation, children felt motivated to write about a social issue (the children were 4 years old). In her book, Vasquez, used the following examples to outline the process of the draft:

> Stefanie had a number of discussions with a group of four other children to decide words to use. "Why don't you say that people need food to live," Melanie suggested. "And, ummm, if you don't eat, you'll die", P.J added. "Should I say 'have to' like it's important?
>
> (Vasquez 2004: 105)

This constructive discourse outlines that children were involved in the clarification of sentence, correct use of tense and the employment of passive and active voices for the purpose of the draft work. This activity was also extended; as a result children began to extend their sentence structure. For example, one child wrote 'Our friend couldn't eat at our barbecue because she/he is a vegetarian and that wasn't fair' (Vasquez 2004: 108). This sentence is clearly a complex sentence and demonstrates the child's intent to make her point clearly. This also indicated that children were aware of the requirements of their work to reflect conventional grammar and structure in the writing process. Therefore, in the task children were reflecting on achieving standards established by the mandated curriculum. Rather than teaching these skills in isolation, children were actively involved in structuring their sentences in the most appropriate way.

Comber (2001: 271) states that, when children participate in critical literacy, they 'ask complicated questions about language and power, about people and life style, about morality and ethics, and about who is advantaged by the way things are and who is disadvantaged'. Comber and Thomson (2001: 456) give the example in which children were asked to draw something that worried them. This activity outlined by Comber and Thomson (see Case study 9.2) enabled children to engage in critical literacy using the principles of critical literacy.

Many academics who write about critical literacy have avoided issues of the use of grammar, phonics and structure of language. One academic who has tried to deal with these issues is Vasquez. In using Vasquez's work, examples will be given of how these objectives based on sentence level can be achieved.

Case study 9.2: The need for water

According to Comber and Thomson (2001), one child responded on a global level focusing on the need for water and other dominant social issues. The child's response was linked to environmental and economic issues within the community. This lesson was extended, as the teacher in the project used the children's concerns to extend discussion by asking probing questions relating to water within their community. In these discussions, 'many children made their concerns known about the poor condition and low number of trees and parks in their neighbourhood' (Comber and Thomson 2001: 257). Other lessons were planned in which the children did fieldwork and research. The topic of water was of importance to these children because they lived in the driest part of South Australia. By highlighting this example, Comber and Thomson (2001) draw attention to the need for literacy to be seen as a form of social practice 'that are part of everyday life in the here and now, part of living in a particular community and attending a particular school'.

Strategies for the implementation of critical literacy

Problem posing

According to McLaughlin and Devoogd (2004b), one strategy that can be used to engage readers with text from a critical literacy perspective is 'problem posing'. Problem posing is a critical literacy strategy that can be used with narrative and informational text, as well as hypertext, a variety of media, and conversation. McLaughlin and DeVoogd's (2004b) idea on 'problem posing' appears similar to a strategy used by Vasquez (2004) called 'problematising social text'. For brevity, McLaughlin and DeVoogd's (2004b) examples will be focused upon. After reading the text, readers engaged in critical literacy questions. Some of these questions, according to McLaughlin and DeVoogd (2004b: 47), could include:

- Who is in the text/picture/situation? Who is missing?
- Whose voices are represented?
- Whose voices are marginalized or discounted?
- What are the intentions of the author? What does the author want the reader to think?
- What would an alternative text/picture/situation say?
- How can the reader use this information to promote equity?

These queries represent high-level questioning that requires children to read the text and respond appropriately. In addition, children are involved in the evaluation and synthesis of reading information. These two features (evaluation and synthesis) can be linked to Bloom's Taxonomy (Bloom et al. 1964) which suggests that educators should strive to develop children to higher levels of cognitive processing. By using these questions or altering them, the teacher could go beyond the mandates of the curriculum.

Setting switch, emotional switch and ethnic/race switch

McLaughlin and DeVoogd (2004b: 47–48) suggest that teachers can be creative in their approach to teaching critical literacy by utilizing the following strategies: 'gender switch', 'theme switch', 'setting switch', 'emotional switch' and 'ethnic/race switch'. Three examples from McLaughlin and Devoogd (2004b) will be highlighted for the purpose of this research. First, 'setting switch' is a strategy that requires children to read a story and then they are asked to change the setting. The changes could reflect the 'time, place and social class' (McLaughlin and DeVoogd, 2004b: 47). The second strategy is 'emotional switch'. According to McLaughlin and DeVoogd (2004b: 48) this could include 'Reimagine a story in which the characters have different emotions tone. The third strategy to be outlined is 'ethnic/race switch', where children could be asked, 'What if the characters were given different ethnic and racial characteristics?' (McLaughlin and DeVoogd 2004b: 48). For example, after reading the story children could be guided to replace the characters with other characters linked to other ethnic and racial characteristics. This activity could also be extended to gender and could develop further critical discussion.

Immersion

The issue of problem posing (McLaughlin and DeVoogd 2004b) and problematizing text (Vasquez 2004) seems to be connected to the concepts of 'immersion' and engagement of text, as outlined by Douglas and Hargadon (2001). According to Douglas and Hargadon (2001), immersion is children's commitment to issues within the text, whereas engagement involves the ability of children. Critical literacy requires active engagement (Lave and Wenger 1991;

Wertsch et al. 1995). This engagement connects the teacher with his or her children. Comber and Nixon (2005: 130) suggest: 'To take a critical approach requires that teachers and children begin to closely examine the text that they read and practice'. These approaches could bring the reader closer to the examination of reading text.

Photo juxtapositioning

The final strategy to be linked with talk is 'photo juxtapositioning'. McLaughlin and DeVoogd (2004b) described photo juxtapositioning as the utilization of two different photos to 'demonstrate different views'. McLaughlin and DeVoogd (2004b) used the example of Michael Gress:

> A middle school teacher juxtaposed two photographs that appeared on the front page of two different American newspapers before the United States went to war in Afghanistan. One photo showed a seven-year-old boy staring into the camera, raising a pistol in the air while sitting on a man's shoulder ... The other photo showed a six-year-old Afghani boy running away, carrying his one-year-old sister on his back looking over his shoulder in fear.
> (McLaughlin and DeVoogd 2004b: 51)

By juxtapositioning the photos, the teacher can stimulate discussion. According to McLaughlin and Devoogd (2004b), these pictures allowed children to understand that photos and texts are not neutral and represent the perspective of the photographer. Within this examination, the issue of power can also be discussed.

Potential tensions within critical literacy

There are certain tensions as teachers use critical literacy. These tensions can be linked to the curriculum. Teachers who engage in critical literacy are sometimes concern regarding curriculum and critical literacy. Many teachers view the curriculum as priority; as a result they will not engage in critical literacy. Nevertheless, I would like to suggest that critical literacy should not be seen as a replacement for any learning framework or curriculum as it enhances the learning competences of children as teacher 'negotiate' (Vasquez 2004) beyond the curriculum when critical literacy is used. Having an understanding of what is a negotiated curriculum will reduce tension between teachers and line managers, parents and teachers, and policymakers and educators.

Conclusion

In this chapter I have highlighted the possibilities for critical literacy within early years. I have proposed seven features of critical literacy that could be used as a method implementing and assessing critical literacy within the curriculum. In highlighting these features it will be important for practitioners to receive relevant training to ensure they are aware of the risk involved in undertaking critical literacy within early years. While some individuals might say that the children in early years should not engage in critical literacy, there are enormous benefits if children are allowed to develop critical thinking skill early using the Freirean perspective of critical literacy. It is possible that a critical literacy designed curriculum could allow for greater creativity from children and teachers. This could lead to a curriculum that is guided by children's interests rather than a political agenda associated with meeting targets and goals. Furthermore, a critical literacy curriculum could establish greater links with the social and cultural issues within children's lives.

Suggested further reading

Freire, P. (1973) *Education for Critical Consciousness*. New York: Seabury.

Freire, P. and Macedo, D. (1987) *Literacy: Reading the word and the world*. London: Bergin & Garvey.

Shor, I. and Pari, C. (2006) *Critical Literacy in Action*. Portsmouth, NH: Heinemann.

References

Aronowitz, S. (1993) 'Paulo Freire's radical democratic humanism.' In P. McLaren and P. Leonard (eds) *Paulo Freire: A critical encounter*. New York: Routledge.

Beck, A. (2005) 'A place for critical literacy.' *Journal of Adolescent and Adult Literacy*, 48(5): 392–400.

Bizzell, P. and Herzberg, B. (1996) *Negotiating Difference: Cultural case studies for composition*. Boston, MA: Bedford.

Bloom, B., Mesia, B. and Krathwohl, D. (1964) *Taxonomy of Education Objectives*. New York: David McKay.

Comber, B. (2001) 'Critical literacies and local action: Teacher knowledge and a "new" research agenda.' In B. Comber and A. Simpson (eds) *Negotiating Critical Literacies in Classrooms*. Mahwah, NJ: Lawrence Erlbaum Associates.

Comber, B. (2004) 'Children reread and rewrite their local neighbourhoods: Critical literacies and identity work.' In J. Evans (ed.) *Literacy Moves On: Using popular culture, new technologies and critical literacy in the primary classroom*. London: David Fulton.

Comber, B. and Nixon, H. (2005) 'Children re-read and re-write their neighbour-hoods: Critical literacies and identity work.' In J. Evans (ed.) *Literacy Moves On: Using popular culture, new technologies and critical literacy in the primary classroom.* Portsmouth, NH: Heinemann.

Comber, B. and Thomson, P. (2001) 'Critical literacy finds a place: Writing and social action in a low-income Australian grade 2/3 Classroom.' *The Elementary School Journal*, 101(4): 451–464.

Cummins, J. and Sayers, D. (1995) *Brave New Schools: Challenging cultural illiteracy through global learning network.* New York: St Martin's Press.

Department for Education and Skills (DfES) (2007) *The Early Years Foundation Stage.* London: DfES

Douglas, J., and Hargadon, A. (2001) 'The pleasures of immersion and engagement: schemas, scripts, and the fifth business.' *Digital Creativity*, 12(3): 153–166.

Dyson, A.H. (1998) 'Folk processes and media creatures: Reflections on popular culture for literacy educators.' *The Reading Teacher*, 51(5): 392–402.

Freire, P. (1970) *Pedagogy of the Oppressed.* New York: Penguin.

Freire, P. (1973) *Education for Critical Consciousness.* New York: Seabury.

Freire, P. (1993) *Pedagogy of the City.* New York: Continuum.

Freire, P. (2005) *Teachers as Cultural Workers: Letters to those who dare to teach.* Trans. D. Macedo, D. Koike and A. Oliveira. Boulder, CO: Westview.

Freire, P. and Macedo, D. (1987) *Literacy: Reading the word and the world.* London: Bergin & Garvey.

Gambrell, L., Palmer, B., Coding, R. and Mozzoni, S. (1996) 'Assessing motivation to read.' *The Reading Teacher*, 49(7): 518–533.

Gee, J. (1990) *An Introduction to Discourse Analysis: Theory and method.* New York: Routledge.

Hannon, P. (2007) 'The history and future of literacy.' In T. Grainger (ed.) *The RoutledgeFalmer Reader in Language and Literacy.* New York: RoutledgeFalmer.

Janks, H. (2000) 'Domination, access, diversity and design: A synthesis for critical literacy.' *Education Review*, 52(2): 175–185.

Jowallah, R. (2010) 'Critical literacy in England: Utilising critical literacy pedagogy with the English National Curriculum at Key Stage Three.' Unpublished EdD thesis, University of Sheffield.

Kretovics, R. (1985) 'Critical literacy: Challenging the assumptions of mainstream educational theory.' *Journal of Education*, 167(2): 50–62.

Kucer, S. (2005) *Dimensions of Literacy: A conceptual base for teaching reading and writing in school settings*, 2nd edn. Mahwah, NJ: Lawrence Erlbaum Associates.

Lankshear, C., with Gee, J.P., Knobel, M. and Searle, C. (1997) *Changing Literacies.* Buckingham: Open University Press.

Larson, J. and Marsh, J. (2005) *Making Literacy Real: Theories and practices for learning and teaching.* London: Sage.

Lave, J. and Wenger, E. (1991) *Situated Learning: Legitimate peripheral participation.* Cambridge: Cambridge University Press.

Lewison, M., Flint, A.S. and Van Sluys, K. (2002) 'Taking on critical literacy: The journey of newcomers and novices.' *Language Arts*, 79(5): 382–392.

Luke, A. and Freebody, A. (1999) *A Map of Possible Practices: Further notes on the four resources model.* Available at www.readingonline.org/research/lukefreebody.html (accessed 3 January 2008).

McLaughlin, M. (2001) 'Sociocultural influences on content literacy teachers' beliefs and innovation practices.' Paper presented at Fifty-first annual meeting of the National Reading Conference, San Antonio, TX, December.

McLaughlin, M. and DeVoogd, G. (2004a) 'Critical literacy as comprehension: Expanding reader response critical literacy helps teachers and students expand their reasoning, seek out multiple perspectives, and become active thinkers.' *Journal of Adolescent and Adult Literacy*, 48(1): 52–62.

McLaughlin, M. and DeVoogd, G. (2004b) *Critical Literacy: Enhancing students' comprehension of text.* New York: Scholastic.

Marsh, J. (1999) 'Batman and Batwoman go to school: Popular culture in the literacy curriculum.' *International Journal of Early Years Education*, 7(2): 117–131.

Meacham, S.J. (2003) *Literacy and 'Street Credibility': Plantations, prisons and African American literacy from Frederick Douglass to Fifty Cent.* Sheffield: University of Sheffield.

Morgan, W. (1997) *Critical Literacy in the Classroom: The art of the possible.* New York: Routledge.

O'Brien, J. (2001) 'Children reading critically: A local history.' In B. Comber and A. Simpson (eds) *Negotiating Critical Literacies in Classrooms.* Mahwah, NJ: Lawrence Erlbaum Associates.

Pompe, C. (1996) '"But they're pink!" – "Who cares!": Popular culture in the primary years.' In M. Hilton (ed.) *Potent Fictions: Children's literacy and the challenge of popular culture.* London: Routledge.

Stribling, S. (2008) 'Using critical literacy practices in the classroom.' *New England Reading Association*, 44(1): 34–38.

Vasquez, V. (2001) 'Constructing a critical curriculum with young children.' In B. Comber and A. Simpson (eds) *Negotiating Critical Literacies in Classrooms.* Mahwah, NJ: Lawrence Erlbaum Associates.

Vasquez, V. (2004) *Negotiating Critical Literacies with Young Children.* Mahwah, NJ: Lawrence Erlbaum Associates.

Wertsch, J., del Rio, P. and Alvarez, A. (1995) 'History, action and mediation.' In J. Wertsch, P. del Rio and A. Alvarez (eds) *Sociocultural Studies of the Mind.* Cambridge: Cambridge University Press.

10 Foucault: implications for multiagency working in the changing landscape of children's services

Maggie Leese

Introduction

Foucault (1926–1984) was a French philosopher well known for his discussions of power, knowledge and discourse where his focus was on studies of social institutions, including the prison system and psychiatry. Foucault is often associated with structuralist, poststructuralist and postmodernist views but he rejected these labels, suggesting that his work should be used by others as tools that could be applied to a range of situations. He was well known for a number of texts including *Madness and Civilization*, *The Birth of the Clinic* and *The Archaeology of Knowledge*.

In this chapter I discuss how I applied Foucault's concepts of knowledge and power (Foucault 1972, 1977) to analyse the research data that I collected over two years in two different Sure Start children's centres. I explore Foucault's discussion of 'discourse' and his suggestion that these discourses operate within 'regimes of truth' (Foucault 1972, 1977; MacNaughton 2005) and I apply them to the practices within children's centres.

I was interested in the way that workers, from a range of professional backgrounds, negotiate their roles when engaging with parents in receipt of family support services, and with other professionals within the changing landscape of children's services (Weinberger 2005). Foucault (1994) proposed an interesting link between power and knowledge, and picking up on this, MacNaughton (2005) highlighted the role of the early years professional in 'uncovering what is invisible' within professional practice as the first step in challenging oppressive practice within early childhood settings. In this chapter I extend the points made by MacNaughton (2005) and apply them to working with families in the community.

Changes in policy and legislation including *Every Child Matters* (DfES 2003) and the Children Act (DfES 2004) have meant a move towards integrated approaches to supporting families, with a shift in focus from dealing with the consequences of difficulties in children's lives, to early intervention and effective prevention. Services delivered by Sure Start children's centres are a direct response to the current political agendas, including reducing child poverty and promoting social inclusion (Wasoff and Cunningham-Bailey 2005). These changes have also led to increased intervention in family life and I draw on Foucault's discussion of the 'Panopticon', initially described by Jeremy Bentham in 1785, a prison where you can be observed without being aware (Foucault 1980a). The idea behind the design of the Panopticon (which was never built) was that prisoners knew that they could be observed at any time, with or without their knowledge; they would therefore learn to regulate their own behaviour in case they were being observed (Foucault 1977). This concept was helpful when I was considering the impact of increased surveillance on families, especially when there were concerns about child protection.

Foucault's ideas about power, knowledge and truth

This chapter does not discuss the complexity of Foucault's work but focuses on his suggestion that power, knowledge and truth operate within 'discourses' (Foucault 1980a, 1980b) and considers how having an understanding of this concept offers professionals an opportunity to reflect critically on their practice (MacNaughton 2005). Foucault (1980a) suggests that a 'discourse' is a particular way of talking about a subject that can take the form of writing, language and thinking and therefore can be very influential in everyday practices within society. Foucault proposed that there are certain dominant discourses that appear to be given the 'stamp of truth'; these are often termed 'regimes of truth' and they are usually located within institutions such as schools and hospitals (Foucault 1980b). In view of this it is important for professionals, who are supporting children and their families, to reflect on their practice as we are often unaware of the impact that these discourses can have on the parents and carers (Gergen 2009).

By considering Foucault's suggestion that some discourses are given the 'stamp of truth' within society, it is possible to examine the impact of power within inter-professional working and in the relationships between family support workers and vulnerable parents in the community. Examining the impact of power on these relationships is crucial to promoting anti-oppressive practice (Thompson 2006) by highlighting the impact of dominant discourses within society that can result in some voices being silenced (Philips and Hardy 2002).

The influence of dominant discourses

Discourses can influence the views of individuals; Gergen (2009: 12) suggests that 'generative discourses' offer the opportunity to challenge the taken for granted understandings and open up the possibility of new ways of thinking and representing. The dominant discourse that relates to families has remarkable strength and power (Bernardes 1990) and usually favours traditional family forms, as Robinson (2006: 85) proposes: 'the nuclear family is the dominant or normalizing discourse of family that operates in western societies'. These discourses about the 'ideal family' are perpetuated through social policy (Driver and Martell 2002) and dissipate down through practice guidelines and are embedded within professional training, leading to what Welland (2001) describes as a 'professional habitus'. In addition to this there can be a discordance between the professionals' own experience of 'family' and the practices that they observe within the families they work with, at times leading to communication difficulties and misunderstandings.

Cultural influences are also important because as Robinson (2006: 82) suggests, there is still a dominant discourse that normalizes the traditional nuclear family based on 'western white, middle class, Christian values and morals'. The impact of this can be significant for families who do not reflect these norms or uphold similar values, resulting in them being excluded or 'othered' because they do not fit with the dominant discourse.

Using concepts from Foucault for data analysis

In my own research I used Foucault's ideas in a number of ways at different stages of the study: initially I spent six months visiting a children's centre and attended both formal and informal meetings. During this time I took an ethnographic approach to my study and by keeping a field diary I was able to analyse the impact of discourses on the professionals who were striving to find 'new ways of working' within children's services. Following this I spent a further year engaging with parents, mostly mothers, who were accessing services within the second children's centre. I used the concepts of power and discourse as a way of analysing the relationships within the centre and also as a tool to consider how the social construction of the 'good enough' parent impacted on the parents' perception of self and their identity.

Negotiating new ways of working

Foucault (1980b) suggested that some forms of knowledge are treated differently, resulting in what is termed 'subjugated knowledge', types of knowledge that are viewed as less important than scientific knowledge. An example of this could be where medical knowledge is given more weight than the views of the nursery worker within an inter-agency team meeting. Foucault's supposition that certain knowledge is favoured over other forms of knowledge is an important factor to consider, especially in relation to inter-agency working where 'truths' of one profession may carry more status than those of another profession. This also requires workers from different professions to find some 'common ground'.

MacNaughton (2005) makes the point that workers need to consider which 'regimes of truth' are impacting on their area of practice and this is crucial because of the circular relationship between these 'regimes of truth' and power. It could be suggested that family support work is based on a 'regime of truth' about child-rearing practices; where a parent or carer makes choices outside of these 'truths' professionals can become concerned. By questioning what knowledge has been disqualified by this process, it is possible to uncover embedded practices that can discriminate against certain groups within society and through this uncovering it is possible for alternative discourses to re-emerge (Foucault 1980b; MacNaughton 2005).

It is possible to use the concepts outlined by Foucault to analyse the way that a range of professionals find ways to work together despite their differences. More and more emphasis has been put on all agencies working in a joined-up way, but the degree to which this is happening on the ground is still open for debate as discussed in the serious case reviews for children such as Baby Peter (Haringey Local Safeguarding Board 2009). Within children's services there is a number of ways that inter-agency teams are located, including co-location where all agencies are based within the same locality, a central team based within a central location that draws on other agencies based in the local area and teams that are based within different locations. This is an important consideration because the way the professionals are located will have an impact on how they work together as an inter-agency team.

Some of the workers that I met felt very strongly that having a range of professionals housed within one building was the best model to promote and sustain inter-professional working, but others felt that it was more about a willingness to communicate and share information, regardless of location. The brief discussion below captures some of the tensions that workers expressed when asked about the move to integrated working.

Family support manager:	It's all right housing them [other agencies] in a building but they can still work in an individual way.
Centre manager:	It is much more about what language we use and being prepared to see things from the perspectives of others...that is difficult for some workers who have been in their job for years.
Centre worker:	I think the difficulty is going to be when we try and mainstream more services as we are trying to do now and there are people in their professional silos. They [the health visitors] don't want to know about these new ways of working, they're quite happy as they are thank you very much. I think that is going to be the challenge for us all.

The key to finding ways to work together appears to be tied up with the need for a common language as identified by Tough (2005) and Salmon and Faris (2006). In addition to this there needs to be an understanding of different values and respect for each area of the children's workforce (Edwards and Gillies 2004; Robinson et al. 2005). It is not surprising that these new ways of working are difficult to achieve because each professional will have experienced different training, leading to what Welland (2001) described as a 'professional habitus'.

The professionals who worked within the children's centre expressed concern about working with colleagues from other disciplines, but they were mostly concerned about working with staff from the National Health Service, because they viewed them as a powerful group. This links back to Foucault's (1980b) discussion about scientific knowledge being given the 'stamp of truth' leading to a perception, by both the parents and other workers, that health care staff are the experts. The discussion below took place following a meeting between health visitors and centre staff to discuss an initiative designed to teach young mothers about healthy eating.

Nursery worker: It won't work with the families from that estate because they are really sick of initiatives and they see right through them . . . I know because I live there.

Nursery manager: You should have said something to the health visitors, told them that they have seen all this before.

Nursery worker: No way, what would they think of me if they know I live on the estate and anyway they are professionals so they are not interested in what I have got to say.

Using Foucault's concepts of power and subjugated knowledge to analyse this exchange we see that the nursery worker had useful knowledge to contribute to the discussion; however, she appears inhibited, first by a perception that the health visitors' knowledge has higher status than hers, and second, that her home address would be viewed by the health visitors as a negative attribute. By not challenging these assumptions, the nursery manager contributes to the ongoing perception that the health visitors' knowledge is of higher status.

By looking at these two brief discussions it is possible to apply the concepts outlined by Foucault to consider the discourses which may influence the professionals within their work. It was clear that the workers viewed the health staff as a powerful group, perhaps because of their link to scientific knowledge, and this was impacting on their ability to work together. There was a lack of challenge from the centre staff even when they did not think the initiative was appropriate because they viewed the health visitors as 'professionals', leading to an assumption that they were more powerful.

Are some parents hard-to-reach?

Foucault's ideas can also be used to analyse the impact of the changes in policy and practice that have resulted in a growing expectation that some parents, including single parents, teenage mothers and asylum-seeking families, will engage in services to support them. Where these excluded groups do not access services, there is the potential that they will be labelled 'hard-to-reach'. Below is a discussion between staff and volunteers in a Sure Start children's centre that illustrates how labelling and issues of power can impact on parents when accessing services.

Community volunteer:	People always talk about the 'hard-to-reach' but no one really knows if families are being missed or if they are just making their own decision not to get support. Parents that won't engage are mainly the sort of families that have some history with social services.
Centre manager:	Yes but we shouldn't be assuming that everybody from a disadvantaged area needs support . . . lots of people need support in lots of different ways.
Family support manager:	The problem is that some of the parents, especially the teenage parents, don't engage because of the appearance of the building. It looks very formal, that's why we do a lot in the community in the dusty old hall . . . they like it there. I think they expect to be told what to do when they come in the centre, they don't want professionals making decisions about how they care for the children. They will ask when they want support.
Family support worker:	We try and break it all down, once you get them into a group or they let you through the front door after a month it seems to be a lot easier. The first part is the hardest because they have to get to know you and then they will put the barriers down.

This exchange was repeated in different forms a number of times within all the centres as the workers struggled to find new ways of engaging families. This brief exchange raises a number of issues relating to power and the way that some families are labelled as 'hard-to-reach' simply because they choose not use the support services that are offered (Edwards and Gillies 2004). There can be a number of reasons that parents do not access services but the issues of power need to be considered especially in relation to working-class mothers who are often labelled as resistant and Gillies (2008) makes the point that the experience of these working-class mothers needs to be explored. By considering which discourses are at play within this discussion, it could suggest that the centre manager was very aware of the labels and the stereotypical views that are attached to some parents and she was keen to dispel these. The volunteer had previously accessed the services at the centre and she made the suggestion that some people's reluctance to engage was related to a 'fear of social services'. This fear of involvement with social services relates to the issue of increased surveillance; families who are involved are likely to experience a greater level of intervention from statutory services and this can have a lasting impact.

This increased level of surveillance for excluded groups can be linked to Foucault's (1977) discussion of a 'Panopticon', a design for a building where people can be observed at all times, therefore allowing access to all aspects of an individual's life. This level of surveillance can be experienced by families when social services have concerns about child safety and in these circumstances parents can start to police their own behaviour in line with the prevailing discourse (Foucault 1999). Parents under scrutiny rarely challenge the level of surveillance that they experience because it becomes internalized; Gergen (2009) suggests that when this happens people will seek to change their behaviour in order to conform.

This idea that parents will start to regulate their own behaviour was evident with the stories that James and Zoe told.

Case study 10.1: James and Zoe

James and his wife Zoe were working hard to keep their children after previously having two other children removed; Zoe was now engaging with support services after suffering a depression that led her to ask social services to take her children. The comment below from James illustrates the impact of the increased surveillance on his family life:

James: I felt like we were fish in a bowl, someone always looking at you . . . I don't think of it like that now because I have made an effort to work with them . . . they are better as friends than enemies.

James had previously had two children removed from his care a number of years ago and the experience of that was clearly still impacted on the way he and his wife now engage with support services. In an effort to 'do things the right way', James has started to change the way he is caring for his children to ensure that it is viewed positively by any professionals that become involved.

In a similar way Zoe had also experienced statutory involvement in her family when she threatened to kill her children because of the depression she was experiencing. Zoe recalled the feelings of helplessness during this period in her life and she now works hard to ensure that she is viewed as a 'good mother'. Zoe admits that she was once a 'nightmare' but she describes how over time she has changed the way she does things to ensure it is the 'right way'.

Zoe: I guess at least they know what they get with me, I tell it how it is but I also know I have to do things properly, the right way, I know that now. I love my kids and I don't ever want to be in that situation again . . . the point where I might lose them forever.

Within both of these stories there is evidence that these parents had started to change their behaviour even though the level of surveillance had decreased. This can be linked to Foucault's (1977) discussion of the 'Panopticon'. This point is also extended by the manager who suggests that the main barrier that remains is the connection that the parents make between support services and the work of social services.

Family support manager: I do say to the social services and the managers that we don't want the Sure Start service to be used as part of a child protection plan because you are putting a different light on Sure Start but very often they do.

These short extracts demonstrate that the children's centre team were working hard to ensure that parents did not connect their support service with intervention under a child protection plan, but for the parents that I spent time with, they rarely differentiated between social services and family support because they viewed them all as 'professionals'. Where parents are under pressure to conform and under constant scrutiny by surveillance from professionals, they appear to respond in different ways. Some change their parenting practice in response to professional views (Gillies 2008) while others simply 'play the game' without challenging the dominant discourse (Hunter 2004).

The social construction of the 'good enough' parent

By using the concepts identified by Foucault, it is possible to reflect on practice in order to identify how the dominant discourses about 'families', including what it means to be a 'good enough' parent, impacts on the services that are offered to support children and families. It can be difficult for families to challenge these ideal views or to identify alternative or submerged understandings that would support their views or choices, because of the strength of the dominant discourse (Millei 2005).

Winnicott (1965) first coined the term 'good enough' mother where he categorized different functions of a mother with a young child, including her ability to hold and handle the infant. This idea was extended by Bettelheim (1988) where he also described the 'good enough' parent as being responsive to the child's needs; this concept has become part of the rhetoric surrounding inter-agency working with children and families and it often represents a deficit model of parenting that can result in parents feeling inadequate. The issue of how professionals define 'good enough' parenting is important and requires them to have a shared understanding of what this concept means (DfES 2004) but, although this term is widely used within policy and practice documents, defining what 'good enough' parenting looks like can be problematic. Although initially the term 'good enough' represented a positive view of parenting, Daniel (2000) questions if it is actually a deficit model, a description of parenting that is far less than the optimum.

In addition to this, the ideology behind the government's plans for supporting families depicts parenting as an occupation that requires expert advice and training, rather than an intimate relationship (Edwards and Gillies 2004), leading to assumptions that the professional is the expert. With this has come increased concern about managing 'risk', placing the spotlight on parents' capacity to meet their child's needs, with an expectation that professionals will work together to support them.

As highlighted earlier, the definition of 'good enough' parenting varies according to policy, professional or personal opinion (Miller and Sambell 2003), which can pose a problem for parents and professionals if their perspectives differ. To investigate this issue within my own research, I focused on how professionals and parents 'tell' and then 'retell' their stories about 'parenting' and being 'parented'. From these data it was possible to identify the discourses that were informing the parents' or carers' understanding, and the professionals' collective understanding of what 'good enough' parenting looks like. The views of the parents and professionals changed over time and from one conversation to another, supporting the suggestion that 'good enough' parenting is a social construct (Gergen 2009) that remains a contested term.

When referring to the care of children, government policy applies the gender-neutral term of parenting rather than 'mothering', but Gillies (2005) proposes that this disguises the fact that mothers still maintain prime responsibility for day-to-day care of the children. Increasingly literature refers to 'parents' rather than 'mothers' but provision of services within children's centres are still designed predominantly to meet the needs of women as the main caregivers, and where services are provided for men, they are often 'separate' from the provision for mothers. Robinson (2006) proposes that the discourse that surrounds the 'good mother' defines motherhood as natural and requires all mothers to be highly attentive and sensitive, a recurrent theme within the stories told by the researched parents and professionals when describing a 'good parent'.

The young mothers within my study were aware of the negative stereotypical view of teenage mothers but they rejected this view and described becoming a mother as a 'turning point' in their life, an opportunity to do the right thing. Kirkman et al. (2001) similarly noted that teenage mothers were reluctant to discuss any negative aspects of their role and they also attempted to 'rewrite' their story so that they could be viewed as 'good enough'. The teenage mothers within both the study by Kirkman et al. (2001) and my own research accepted the 'good enough' parent discourse and attempted to tell 'their story' to fit with and the dominant discourse, without attempting to challenge it. Hunter (2004) makes the point that by attempting to conform to a dominant discourse of 'good enough' mothering, or in Foucault's terms by not challenging the 'regimes of truth', they are in fact strengthening the very structures and systems that oppress them.

Furthermore, by considering Foucault's concept of 'subjugated knowledge' we can grasp a deeper understanding of some parents' reluctance to follow professional advice on parenting, particularly if this advice clashed with the parents' cultural norms of child-rearing. The parents may feel that their own knowledge of child-rearing is of less worth than the 'expert' knowledge of professionals and therefore their knowledge is subjugated. My research data show that many mothers find it difficult to ignore suggestions made by the professionals and many of the mothers in the study expressed concern that if they did ignore the advice, they would be viewed as being a 'bad parent'. Thus the professional discourse of 'good' mothering normalizes certain behaviours (such as breastfeeding) and although there is no uncontested definition of 'good' mothering parents feel obliged to conform. The quote below demonstrates how Gemma struggled to negotiate between the dominant discourse that encouraged her to breastfeed and her experience within her own family.

Case study 10.2: Gemma

Gemma: I hate seeing new mums breastfeeding because when I had my baby the workers said I should breastfeed but my mum and granny were dead against it. When I see the workers supporting the girls that are breastfeeding, I know that I will never be as good a mum as they are.

Clearly Gemma had absorbed the professional messages that breastfeeding contributes to 'good' mothering and she was concerned that she would be labelled as a 'bad' mother by the professionals. Her family had discouraged her from breastfeeding, but she has now become aware that her choice is not in line with the professional discourse. Gemma's child is now 3 years old but she still feels that the staff at the centre will judge her based on her decision not to breastfeed and in our discussions she is able to recall a number of exchanges where she has felt 'guilty' for not breastfeeding.

> **Gemma:**   One day I went to the doctors because he had a bad chest and the first thing that he asked was if he was breastfed...I went out of the doctors and all I could think was that it was my fault that he was sick...but babies that are breastfed get sick as well but I guess 'cos I am young and a single parent he [the doctor] just made assumptions about me.

Although Gemma is able to rationalize and understands that all babies are susceptible to colds during the winter months, she feels that because she is young and single she is more vulnerable to being labelled as a 'bad' mother.

This was a theme that was evident in a number of the stories that the mothers told and many of them felt that they were being 'pulled in different directions' by a conflict between the professionals' view and the views of their families.

Parents like Gemma can experience a disjuncture between their own cultural narrative and the narrative of the 'good' mother; this can impact on their 'perception of self' (Goffman 1959) and can result in a lack of self-esteem. Gemma often talked about the way that she felt she was living two separate lives, one at home where it was normal to smoke, drink and take drugs and the other life at the centre, where she aspired to do the best for her child and strived to be what she described as 'the best mum'. This was the experience of most of the young mothers who I met during the study; this personal conflict resulted in the mothers feeling that they do not 'belong' or that their parenting practices do not fit with the ethos of either the children's centre or their own family environment. This can impact on the crucial identity development of a 'good' mother for, as Croghan and Mielle (1998) point out, they may avoid engaging with professionals for fear of being viewed as a 'bad parent' and therefore stigmatized.

In conclusion this chapter has outlined how we can use Foucauldian concepts to reflect on practice within children's services. By using these concepts as a tool within research, it is possible to analyse the stories that people tell about their lived experiences and this can then inform future practice. I was able to use Foucault's central ideas about power to inform my discussion on issues including the social construction of the 'good enough' parent, the increase in surveillance and the labelling of parents as 'hard to reach' and the difficulties that are inherent within the move to integrated working.

Implications for practice

From my own study and the other studies discussed, there are a number of points that can support professionals in becoming critically reflective about their practice.

- Issues of power are inherent in the relationships between different professionals and these needs to be considered in order to move to more integrated ways of working.
- The relationships that workers form with parents take time to establish and professionals need to understand that they are often viewed as the 'expert'.
- When working with children and families it is important to be aware of dominant discourses that are informing the service provision.
- Certain groups, including working-class families and teenage mothers, are subject to increasing levels of surveillance and if they do not access the support that is offered they often find themselves labelled as 'hard-to-reach'.
- It is important for professionals to understand how their individual engagement with families can have a lasting impact on the identity of the parents.

Suggested further reading

Gordan, C. (ed.) (1980) *Power / Knowledge: Selected interviews and other writings 1972–1977*. Brighton: Harvester.
MacNaughton, G. (2005) *Doing Foucault in Early Childhood*. London: Routledge.
Weinberger, J., Pickstone, C. and Hannon, P. (eds) (2005) *Learning from Sure Start: Working with young children and their families*. Maidenhead: Open University Press.

References

Bernardes, J. (1990) 'The family in question.' *Social Studies Review*, 6(1): 33–35.
Bettelheim, B. (1988) *Good Enough Parent: A book on child rearing*. New York: Random House.
Croghan, R. and Mielle, D. (1998) 'Strategies of resistance: "Bad" mothers dispute the evidence.' *Feminism and Psychology*, 8(4): 445–465.
Daniel, B. (2000) 'Judgements about parenting: What do social workers think they are doing'? *Child Abuse Review*, 9(2): 91–107.
DfES (2003) *Every Child Matters: Change for Children*. London: HMSO.
DfES (2004) *The Children Act*. London: HMSO.
Driver, S. and Martell, L. (2002) 'New Labour, work and the family.' *Social Policy and Administration*, 36(1): 46–61.
Edwards, R. and Gillies, V. (2004) Support in parenting: Values and consensus concerning who to turn to. *Journal of Social Policy*, 33(4): 623–643.
Foucault, M. (1972) *The Archaeology of Knowledge*. London: Tavistock.

Foucault, M. (1977) *Discipline and Punish: The Birth of the Prison.* New York: Pantheon.

Foucault, M. (1980a) 'Truth and power.' In C. Gordan (ed.) *Power / Knowledge: Selected interviews and other writings 1972–1977.* Brighton: Harvester.

Foucault, M. (1980b) 'Two lectures.' In C. Gordan (ed.) *Power / Knowledge: Selected interviews and other writings 1972–1977.* Brighton: Harvester.

Foucault, M. (1994) *Power: Essential works of Foucault 1954–1984.* London: Penguin.

Foucault, M. (1999) 'Disciplinary power and subjection.' In S. Lukes (ed.) *Power.* Oxford: Basil Blackwell.

Gergen, K.J. (2009) *An Invitation to Social Construction.* London: Sage.

Gillies, V. (2005) 'Meeting parents' needs? Discourses of "support" and "inclusion" in family policy.' *Critical Social Policy,* 25(1): 70–90.

Gillies, V. (2008) 'Perspectives on parenting responsibility: Contextualizing values and practice.' *Journal of Law and Society,* 35(1): 95–112.

Goffman, E. (1959) *The Presentation of Self in Everyday Life.* St Ives: Clays.

Haringey Local Safeguarding Board (2009) *Serious Case Review: Baby Peter. Executive Summary.* Available at www.haringeylscb.org/executive_summary_peter_final.pdf (accessed 4 May 2010).

Hunter, L. (2004) 'Bourdieu and the social space of the PE class: Reproduction of doxa through practice.' *Sports Education and Society,* 9(2): 175–192.

Kirkman, M., Harrison, L., Hillier, L. and Pyett, P. (2001) '"I know I am doing a good job": Canonical and autobiographical narratives of teenage mothers.' *Culture Health and Sexuality,* 3(3): 279–294.

MacNaughton, G. (2005) *Doing Foucault in Early Childhood.* London: Routledge.

Millei, Z.J. (2005) 'The discourse of control: Disruption and Foucault in an early childhood classroom.' *Contemporary Issues in Early Childhood,* 6(2): 128–139.

Miller, S. and Sambell, K. (2003) 'What do parents feel they need? Implications of parents' perspectives for the facilitation of parenting programmes.' *Children and Society,* 17(1): 32–44.

Phillips, N. and Hardy, C. (2002) *Discourse Analysis: Investigating processes of social construction.* London: Sage.

Robinson, K. (2006) *Diversity and Difference in Early Childhood Education.* Maidenhead: Open University Press.

Robinson, M., Anning, A. and Frost, N (2005) '"When is a teacher not a teacher?": Knowledge creation and the professional identity of teachers within multi-agency teams.' *Studies in Continuing Education,* 27(2): 175–192.

Salmon, G. and Faris, J. (2006) 'Multi-agency collaboration, multiple levels of meaning: Social constructionism and the CMM model as tools to further our understanding.' *Journal of Family Therapy,* 28(3): 272–292.

Thompson, N. (2006) *Anti-Discriminatory Practice.* Basingstoke: Palgrave.

Tough, S. (2005) *Common Assessment and the Lead Professionals.* Telford: Telford and Wrekin Borough Council.

Wasoff, F. and Cunningham-Bailey, S. (eds) (2005) *Perspectives on Social Policies and Families*. Bristol: Policy Press.

Weinberger, J. (2005) 'Family support.' In J.C. Weinberger, C. Pickstone and P. Hannon (eds) *Learning from Sure Start: Working with young children and their families*. Maidenhead: Open University Press.

Weinberger, J., Pickstone, C. and Hannon, P. (eds) (2005) *Learning from Sure Start: Working with young children and their families*. Maidenhead: Open University Press.

Welland, T. (2001) 'Living in the "Gaze of the Empire": Time, enclosure and surveillance in a theological college.' *Sociological Review*, 49(1): 117–135.

Winnicott, D.W. (1965) *The Family and Individual Development*. London: Tavistock.

11 Feminism, the ethic of care and professional roles with care settings

Jo Winwood

Introduction

This chapter considers the relevance of the ethic of care to those working within schools, with particular reference to issues of inclusion and special educational needs. Tronto (1993, cited in Day 2000) stipulates that the ethic of care is a model of moral development where notions of care are highly valued, rather than the traditional view of a low status, female-dominated activity, rooted within the personal spheres of the family. For Tronto (1993, cited in Day 2000: 105) care comprises 'everything that we do to maintain, continue and repair our world so that we can live in it as well as possible. Our world includes our bodies, our selves and our environment'. Thus, an ethic of care goes beyond the personal relationships and settings into formal social and political institutions within society.

For my own research into the role of the SENCO, I felt that an ethic of care was judged to be appropriate because, through interviews with special educational needs coordinators, it became clear that they were utilizing the core principles of developing and sustaining personal and professional relationships, so that pupils, staff and parents could work more effectively together. The role of the SENCO is unique in that it is not based upon a curriculum subject. While other coordinators within school, such as a literacy or numeracy coordinator, have an academic subject upon which to base their work, the SENCO role is based on pupils, and this has in turn produced academic research and study. From this perspective, decisions about SEN have to highlight the person, rather than an abstract set of rules or judgements, although these are often seen within SEN, for example, when linked to funding and provision. Within this, the SENCO has to work alongside two core education drivers – inclusion and achievement. These two issues will be explored in relation to the ethic of care.

What is the ethic of care?

The ethic of care was initially developed by the psychologist Carol Gilligan in response to what she believed to be significant weaknesses in the work of Lawrence Kohlberg. Kohlberg had developed a system to measure moral maturity, which produced results that suggested females were less morally mature than their male counterparts. Gilligan (1993: 18) noted that within the research participants used by Kohlberg to develop his theory of moral reasoning, 'females simply do not exist': Kohlberg's work was based on a study that used 84 males and no females. From this research, Kohlberg developed a six-stage sequence of moral development that he claimed to be universally applicable to all people. However, Gilligan (1993) highlighted the fact that members of the groups that were excluded from the initial sample, including women, rarely reached the higher levels of the sequence, often rising no higher than the stage that focuses on interpersonal relationships and working with others. Kohlberg justified this lack of progression by stating that it was due to women's lack of experience outside the home. In the home, it is acceptable to base moral decision-making around building relationships, whereas outside the home, effective decision-making, according to Kohlberg (described in Gilligan 1993), should reflect society's rules and universal principles of justice. Gilligan (1993) suggests that this approach is contradictory in that the traits that are most associated with women – kindness and caring – are then used to identify them as deficient when related to moral reasoning.

In response to the ethic of justice developed by Kohlberg, Gilligan (1993) developed the ethic of care. Within this she noted that men tend to approach moral decision-making from a justice perspective that is based around principles of individual rights, fairness and autonomy whereas women tend to consider the various competing responsibilities they have, such as mother, wife or friend. The ethic of care aims to sustain and develop relationships, focusing on the needs of others and is context bound, rather than aiming to base the decision-making process on abstract notions of rights and rules. As Gilligan (1993: 19) states, 'problems arise from conflicting responsibilities rather than from competing rights and requires for its resolution a mode of thinking that is contextual and narrative rather than formal and abstract'. The origin of this emphasis on care has been linked to early socialization (Chodorow 1978), in that girls often stay attached to their mother as they mature and develop, whereas boys are encouraged to break this connection, so that their masculine identity can develop. According to Chodorow (1978), female identity is based on the relationships and attachments that they create and maintain, whereas male identity is based around individuation.

Although these differences can and have been linked to the sexes, a number of authors, including Gilligan, have suggested that while the underlying traits of each theory are usually observed in the related sex, there will always be numerous examples of men following the principles of the ethic of care and women utilizing the ethic of justice. In this respect, neither the ethic of care nor the ethic of justice is bound to either sex. Furthermore, Tarvis (1992) suggests that the ethic of care outlined by Gilligan was not meant to replace the ethic of justice or suggest that women's moral thinking was in some way superior to men's. It was simply meant to highlight the fact that different people approach moral questions in different ways, but in an ideal situation both justice and caring would be used to aid the decision-making process (Day 2000).

Within current western society, principles of independence, self-sufficiency, self-interest and rights are often stressed above interdependence and support from a wider community (Code 1991). The ethic of justice reflects this, with the purpose of human life to be the realization of individuality (Verkerk 2005). The influence of this can be seen in many aspects of modern society, including the UK education system, with its clear focus on personal achievement, standards and competition between individual pupils and schools. In contrast, the ethic of care is underpinned by notions of connectivity and interdependence on others. Through this development of empathetic and mutually supporting relationships, both the individual and larger group of which they are a part, benefit as well as developing an autonomous self. Autonomy is thus developed through relationships with others, rather than separating ourselves from others (Held 1993).

Case study 11.1: Lorraine (SENCO in a children's centre)

Lorraine works in a children's centre in an area of significant deprivation; many of the pupils have very difficult home lives. As SENCO, Lorraine works with the children, parents, health visitors and midwives, school staff, social workers, educational psychologists, school nurse and a counsellor. Lorraine states that those involved with the scheme can identify a range of benefits, particularly in terms of the responses from each professional, that now complement each other. Children, parents and staff have seen benefits that are educational and social. For example, parents feel much more capable of working with staff, but are also using what they have learned with their other children. This reflects the relational element of the ethic of care.

Within the education system, notions of inclusion and valuing diversity can be seen to reflect principles of an ethic or care, in that inclusion and the ethic of care are about values such as involvement, empathy and holism. This focus on inclusion can be seen in a number of recent policy documents relating to SEN and education generally. Despite current UK policy stressing both inclusion and achievement, some authors (Black-Hawkins et al. 2007) question whether the two concepts, like the ethic of care and the ethic of justice, are compatible. For many teachers and particularly for those working with pupils with SEN, decisions about responses and provision are based around principles of the ethic of care, as it takes into issues that include personal and social development as well as academic progress.

The ethic of care and special educational needs

Inclusion

The notion of inclusion for all pupils, regardless of their diverse learning needs is a relatively recent development within the English education system. The Warnock Committee (DES 1978) and subsequent Education Act 1981 supported the notion of integration for some children who, historically, would have attended an alternative educational provision, usually based on medical diagnosis of impairments rather than educational ability or need. Although this can now be seen as a significant development, integration expects the child or children to conform to the system within which they are placed, rather than the system responding to their individual needs. As Corbett (1996: 196) states, integration is often understood to mean that the child needs to 'become like the majority; conceal your difficulties; learn to fit in'. However, with an increasing awareness of various inequalities within the education system for certain groups of students, the notion of inclusion instead of integration became a guiding principle within government guidance, including the *Special Educational Needs Code of Practice* (DfES 2001b). This change in policy is important in that it not only offers an opportunity to challenge the traditional deficit model of SEN, that has permeated school policy, provision and practice, but also encourages school staff to reconsider their own values and beliefs about children with impairments or SEN. Rather than viewing an impairment as a problem for the individual, the ethic of care would propose the view that each individual is different and there is a recognition and respect for this diversity, what Vogt (2002: 262) terms as 'caring as commitment'; a professional responsibility to children's learning and personal growth.

Case study 11.2: Helen (SENCO in a primary school)

Helen has been a SENCO for over three years. The school is situated within an area of significant disadvantage, and the children have a range of SEN. When she took on the role, staff had an expectation that they would refer children to her and, as SENCO she would be responsible for designing, implementing and reviews any changes in provision. However, due to the number of children identified, Helen could not manage this. Furthermore, she wanted teaching and support staff to become much more involved with the children with SEN, rather than seeing them as a distinct and separate group, reflecting the commitment element of the ethic of care.

Helen worked with staff to develop their skills and confidence in responding to diverse needs. Many of the strategies developed were aimed at particular children but staff quickly saw other children benefiting from the alternative approaches and now see this level of differentiation as a normal part of lesson planning. This was not only beneficial for pupils, but also for staff as they are now much more able to respond to diverse learners within their classroom and identify this as a particular strength of the staff team.

Ainscow et al. (2006) suggest that this move towards inclusion reflects an international drive towards inclusive practice within education, as many governments adopt the principles of the Salamanca statement (cited in Ainscow et al. 2006). However, although everyone working within the education field uses the term 'inclusion', understanding of the term and what it means in terms of practice is not always clear. Booth and Ainscow (2002) reflect the views held by many that inclusion is a journey rather than a destination:

> inclusion is a never-ending process. It is relevant to any school however inclusive or exclusive its current cultures, policies and practices. It requires schools to engage in a critical examination of what can be done to increase the learning and participation of the diversity of students within the school and its locality.
>
> (Booth and Ainscow 2002: 12)

Wall (2003) defines inclusion within the early years as:

> a process by which *all* children can access, at all times, all aspects of the provision. It is not a process in which practitioners welcome a child and adapt the curriculum and/or resources to provide for that child, rather that the inclusive setting will automatically be catering for individual needs and will therefore offer effective provision for every child. Provision will not offer deficit services that adapt to meet the perceived or identified deficits within children but will offer entitlement to all children.
>
> (Wall 2003: 164)

The quotes highlight the essential distinction between inclusion and integration made previously, stressing the need for any childcare setting to routinely respond to a range of different needs, rather than the pupils being expected to change and adapt to the system they are in or staff only developing a range of learning experiences when a particular child presents with a specific need. This principle is stressed in a number of government documents, including *Inclusive Schooling* (DfES 2001a), which highlights the need to identify and remove barriers to learning, linking it to principles of rights for all children and an appropriate educational experience for all. The document makes reference to inclusion both in terms of learning and more broadly as an ability to participate within the life of a school, highlighting the relational element within inclusion, which should start with early years' settings and continue into all aspects of society. This view of inclusion reflects the broad definition of the ethic of care outlined by Verkerk (2005: 136) as 'living well in concrete relationships with others, responding to their needs and building up a joint life.' Verkerk (2005) stresses the need to recognize and respect the particularity of individual pupils and their family, within a wider society that is based on relationships from which everyone benefits.

However, although the notion of inclusion is central to many current educational drivers and debates, it continues to be an ongoing process, with local authorities and schools responding to the challenges in a variety of ways, and with differing levels of success.

Achievement

Running alongside the inclusion drive is an increasing focus on the achievement of pupils within the education system. This issue can be identified by a number of developments in recent years, including the increased testing of children's performances at various points throughout their education career with even the very youngest children being measured and judged against specific criteria as part of the Foundation Stage Profile, as well as the publication of schools performance data in the form of league tables. Ainscow et al. (2006) suggest that this, like inclusion, reflects global changes in education as governments are trying to ensure that the education system is producing a suitably skilled work force that will enable the country to compete within the global economy. Even *Every Child Matters* (DfES 2004a) makes specific reference to 'make a positive contribution and achieve economic well being'. Parsons (1999) highlights the fact that within a relatively short space of time, schools and childcare settings have moved from being the local resource responding to the needs of the children within the surrounding catchment area, to business like corporations that need to attract pupils, through mechanisms such as league tables, in order to increase revenue. Perhaps this development was meant to increase inclusive practice alongside school improvement; as schools and staff develop professional skills and knowledge in order to meet targets set, responding to a diverse range of pupils needs could be an element of this improvement. However, this focus on attainment within the education system highlights some of the values that are being stressed in the political and cultural contexts of society. These include competitiveness and comparison, accountability and the breakup of wider social (including family) support systems in favour of individual gains and needs. Corbett (1999) notes the rise of notions of 'entitlement' within education and particularly SEN, with its focus on individuals getting the resources they need, appears to be in complete contrast to the principles of inclusion, that values everyone, regardless of their needs. Issues of individual rights and autonomy are closely linked to the ethic of justice, in that it emphasizes competing rights of different individuals, rather than competing responsibilities as in the ethic of care.

Ainscow et al. (2006) and Dyson (2001) point out that achievement within the current system has been defined very narrowly in terms of reaching a particular standard by a certain age within a small number of subject areas, all of which are measured and used to judge the effectiveness of the school by various organizations, including Ofsted. These measurements might offer some insights into school effectiveness but, as Grace (1998) stresses, academic results are often only one element of what makes an effective school, and achievement can be measured in various other ways, such as social development and attendance. An evaluation of extended services in schools and children's centres by Ofsted (2006) recognized that the most successful settings were those that were shaped in response to the needs of children and families they were working with, rather than simply implementing national strategies that did not reflect the requirements of their local community. This links to the point raised by Wall (2003) that for inclusion to be successful, early years settings and schools have to develop their provision so that learning opportunities reflect the diverse needs of the group, with staff having a sound knowledge of individual children and their particular needs. In this way, inclusion should not be additional or extra work for staff when a new child arrives, but simply a part of their everyday plans that start with a particular learning objective that is developed to enable all children to achieve it.

The introduction of *Contextual Added Value (CAV) Information* (DfES 2007) has meant that school data now take into account a number of factors that have shown to have an impact on pupil achievement, including 'special educational needs, first language and income deprivation'. Although this could make the league tables more comparable, the measures used are still very narrow. Furthermore, it does little to challenge the culture of competition and the lack of academic success for certain marginalized groups, which are obvious within the current education culture.

Nias (1999) and Vitton and Wasonga (2009) stress the importance of recognizing the culture and values being advocated within schools and childcare settings as these tend to shape the actions, beliefs and views of the staff and pupils. By focusing on individual achievement, education outcomes could be reduced to little more than test scores. In contrast to this, by adopting a 'caring' approach to education enables teachers to promote achievement in the traditional sense of academic attainment and to develop the 'whole pupil' as a member of a wider society. Nias (1999) notes that the relational aspect of an ethic of care should be a fundamental characteristic of anyone working with children and young people because of the importance of making all children feel happy, secure and valued within a classroom is essential if they are to learn, but this can be achieved only through the creation and maintenance of positive and supportive relationships, reflecting key principles of the ethic of care. This can then lead to opportunities for all pupils, and does not limit achievement to a narrow set of exam results (Vogt 2002). Wall (2003) suggests that many children's centres are already creating very inclusive environments, that span education and the local community, with every member being able to offer something, while still having their individual needs met. In this way, they could offer a vision of inclusion, but Wall (2003) stresses that this does not happen without careful reflection on provision, ongoing professional development and an ethos of inclusion being valued by everyone involved. Achievement is still valued but personalized to each individual, rather than confined to national measurements.

This highlights a further issue when considering what achievement is, in that English education systems are still very limited in terms of choice for pupils when choosing possible modes of study often linked to future aspirations. *Removing Barriers to Achievement* (DfES 2004b: 2) states that 'pupils will be able to follow courses which build on their interests and aptitudes and lead to recognized qualifications'. However, only traditional achievements, such as GCSE and A levels, form part of the measurements of achievement by pupils currently and certain elements of the curriculum have often been considered by both educationalists, parents and students as the second rate option, with the traditional A level and degree route as the best way to achieve economic success, as these types of qualifications are valued more highly than vocational qualifications by employers, but for many pupils with SEN, choices and options within the education system have been limited to less valuable elements of the education system and this perpetuates the inequalities they experience in their day-to-day lives (Lloyd 2004; Noddings 2005). By applying principles of an ethic of care to education and achievement, so that education encompassed notions of social responsibility, active citizenship and cooperation as well as personal achievement, inclusion could become a reality for much greater numbers of children and benefit society as a whole. As Carlsson-Paige and Lantieri (2005) suggest, in order to build a cohesive society, schools need to be encouraged to foster compassionate and responsible pupils, who value diversity, as well as developing their cognitive skills. This theme is extended by Vogt (2002) as he noted that teachers and care staff using the principles of the ethic of care within their own classroom highlighted the importance of respect and empathy between each member of the group, which then lead to an ethos of care within that classroom. When this happens, students are no longer judged on the type of qualifications they took, but their overall contribution to the group of which they were a part, reflecting the social experiences of people with SEN before the industrial revolution, where everyone had a role that reflected their own particular skills.

Although there can be little doubt that teachers 'care' about the children in their class, Bennett (2003) points out that teachers are often quite unwilling to take responsibility for any aspect of caring that is not related to the academic element of the role, highlighting a division between those working in childcare settings and schools. The 'early years' spans both of these settings, but the value placed on care seems to be quite different, even though childcare is now the responsibility of the education system in Britain. Cameron et al. (2002) suggest that childcare is viewed as a substitute for mothering, when mothers have to work. They also highlight the low levels of pay and qualifications held by many childcare workers, particularly in comparison to those working with young children as a teacher. This leads to caring being judged as less valuable than formal learning, and as something that requires experience over professional qualifications, reinforcing the role as an extension of mothering, rather than a career. However, Moss (2001) suggests that the ethic of care could underpin the work of every child care worker and teacher, so that they support the development of young children in all aspects of life, not just learning. Cameron et al. (2002) argue that this could transform the current view of childcare workers, moving it from an extension of the mothering role, to a role that complemented the work of parents and schools. Furthermore, Cameron et al. (2002) believe that by changing perceptions of the role of childcare worker, the potential workforce to be drawn from a wider group of people, challenging the over-representation of women in caring roles.

Case study 11.3: Sarah (SENCO in a primary school)

Sarah has been the SENCO at a large primary school for over eight years. The school is in an affluent area, but the success of the Learning Support Unit and because the school has received additional funding to enable pupils with physical impairments to access the building, the background of the pupils is varied and includes children who do not live in the immediate catchment area of the school.

Sarah forced staff to reassess their views of children with SEN by setting targets for them, via Individual Education Plans, which were similar to all other pupils of a similar ability within the classroom. Many teaching staff immediately presumed that children with an impairment would struggle to learn and that they would need a great deal of additional support. However, these views were challenged by the success of the pupils and staff now plan lessons from the learning objective, rather than any impairment a student might have. Individual needs are considered when the learning objective and lesson plan have been outlined. Pupils without SEN also see teaching staff working with and responding to diversity, and this has also developed an inclusive ethos within the school.

The move away from the traditional deficit model in SEN links closely to the model of education advocated by Wedell (2005) that recognizes both the diversity of students and a curriculum that includes 'elements of skills, knowledge, understanding and attitudes', that reflect the interests and strengths of an individual, making educational achievement about much more that scores in national tests. This type of approach would allow schools to focus on the needs of the children in their classrooms, which can be very different to the needs of a national curriculum, such as social and behavioural needs, as well as developing what could be termed academic skills and achievement that specifically relate to the needs of the children. Wedell (2005) highlights that this type of approach has enabled schools to develop inclusive practice and has had positive effects on learning, achievement and relationships within schools. Noddings (2005) supports this view by stating that caring has an element of responding to an expressed need, rather than just presuming that the person caring knows best. She points out that by actively involving pupils in decisions about their education, as well as specifically including the relational aspect of learning in the curriculum, pupils are much more likely to engage with learning for the sake of learning, rather than simply being grade orientated. Furthermore, continual reflection on the overall aims of the education system could, according to Noddings (2005), create a much more equitable education system that is concerned about all of its members.

Weaknesses of the ethic of care

While the ethic of care can provide students and practitioners an opportunity to consider how they are making decisions within their working life, particularly in relation to various other pressures that they have to reconcile these with, including policy expectations and professional judgements. However, as with any theoretical approach, there are a number of weaknesses that need to be explored. Although the ethic of care is identified with feminism, Gilligan (1993: 2) stresses that the ethic of care is not based on gender but theme, and the use of different voices related to the sexes was to 'highlight a distinction between two modes of thought and to focus a problem of interpretation rather than to represent a generalisation of either sex'. The ethic of care is not based on the belief that women are inherently more moral than men or that women are innately caring. Gilligan (1993) goes on to highlight that you need to consider the cultural, social and historical influences on people, when trying to understand how they approach decision-making. Gilligan (1993) was critical of the lack of women in the research Kohlberg used for the ethic of justice. Cockburn (2005) notes that the ethic of care is based on the experiences of white, middle-class women, but many other groups still possess an ethic of care upon which moral decisions are based. Held (1993) and Hurd and Brabeck (1997) refer to research that supports the notion that the ethic of care is not gender based, but often dependent on the involvement of the person making the decision with a particular situation. Hypothetical dilemmas often produce responses that reflect universal principles whereas decisions that would directly impact on a person utilize care and empathy, and aim to maintain relationships. Thus, both men and women can and do use the ethic of care and the ethic of justice.

The term 'care' within the context of education can lack clarity of meaning. Vogt (2002) identifies a range of ways that 'caring' within the education setting could be interpreted, including physical care, commitment and building relationships. Even so, care cannot be used as an excuse for doing something that is morally questionable; caring *per se* is not enough. For example, a teacher allows a child to complete a colouring sheet rather than the written activity in a lesson because the child struggles with written work. He will be happier doing the colouring and will not be embarrassed in front of his friends, who can complete the task. This can be seen to be the 'caring' option, but the long-term impact of such an approach would be far reaching. The caring option here would be for the teacher to enable the child to complete the entire task; perhaps he could record his answer or work with a writing buddy. In this respect caring has to be more than having the right attitude and the ability to empathize with others; action is also required (Dyson 1997). Caring might start from an ideal notion of what should be done in a particular situation but this needs to be translated into concrete acts, where a person takes responsibility and is responsive to the needs of others (Sevenhuijsen 2003).

The ethic of care stresses the importance of relationships, with obvious links to the emotional aspect of life. This relational aspect contrasts with the rule-based approach of the ethic of justice, that is criticized for being too rigid and objective, ignoring the complex nature of society. However, caring for someone does not automatically equip that person with the skills or knowledge needed to make a moral decision, and basing decisions only on our emotions could be as dangerous as always following a rule or principle (Botes 2000). For staff working in early years settings and schools, there is a need to be caring, while retaining some emotional detachment from the children, so that they can make judgements based on professional knowledge and understandings, and not just emotions. Bennett (2003) contrasts the focus on care within early years settings to that of teaching staff, many of whom do not see a caring element within the role of teacher, which for them is about academic attainment and development. Furthermore, when trying to make decisions about children and young people, staff are regularly confronted with the dilemma of what they want to do to enable the child to succeed, but within the confines of a restricted budget, as well as other social or physical barriers. Staff have then to try to provide equitable educational experiences for all pupils, even if this means that their response is not the ideal solution.

Suggested further reading

Carlsson-Paige, N. and Lantieri, L. (2005) 'A changing vision of education.' In N. Noddings (ed.) *Educating Citizens for Global Awareness.* New York: Teachers College Press.

Cockburn, T. (2005) 'Children and the feminist ethic of care.' *Childhood*, 12(2): 71–89.

Vogt, F. (2002) 'A caring teacher: Explorations into primary school teachers' professional identity and ethic of care.' *Gender and Education*, 14(3): 251–264.

References

Ainscow, M., Booth, T. and Dyson, A. (2006) 'Inclusion and the standards agenda: Negotiating policy pressures in England.' *International Journal of Inclusive Education*, 10(4–5): 295–308.

Bennett, J. (2003) 'Starting strong: The persistent division between care and education.' *Journal of Early Childhood Research*, 1: 21–48.

Black-Hawkins, K., Florian, L. and Rouse, M. (2007) *Achievement and Inclusion in Schools.* London: Routledge.

Booth, T. and Ainscow, M. (2002) *Index for Inclusion: Developing learning participation in schools.* Bristol: Centre for Studies on Inclusive Education.

Botes, A. (2000) A comparison between the ethics of justice and the ethics of care. *Journal of Advanced Nursing*, 32(5): 1071–1075.

Cameron, C., Mooney, A. and Moss, P. (2002) 'The child care workforce: Current conditions and future directions.' *Critical Social Policy*, 22: 572–595.

Carlsson-Paige, N. and Lantieri, L. (2005) 'A changing vision of education.' In N. Noddings (ed.) *Educating Citizens for Global Awareness.* New York: Teachers College Press.

Chodorow, N. (1978) *The Reproduction of Mothering.* Los Angeles, CA: University of California Press.

Cockburn, T. (2005) 'Children and the feminist ethic of care.' *Childhood*, 12(2): 71–89.

Code, L. (1991) *What Can She Know? Feminist theory and the construction of knowledge.* Ithaca, NY: Cornell University Press.

Corbett, J. (1999) 'Inclusivity and school culture: The case of special education.' In J. Prosser (ed.) *School Culture*. London: Paul Chapman.

Corbett, J. (1996) *The Language of Special Needs*. London: Falmer.

Day, K. (2000) 'The ethic of care and women's experiences of public space.' *Journal of Environmental Psychology*, 20: 103–124.

Department of Education and Science (DES) (1978) *Special Educational Needs: Report of the Committee of Enquiry into the Education of Handicapped Children and Young People* (Warnock Committee). London: HMSO.

Department for Education and Skills (DfES) (2001a) *Inclusive Schooling*. Nottingham: DfES.

Department for Education and Skills (DfES) (2001b) *Special Educational Needs Code of Practice*. Nottingham: DfES.

Department for Education and Skills (DfES) (2004a) *Every Child Matters: Change for Children*. London: HMSO.

Department for Education and Skills (DfES) (2004b) *Removing Barriers to Achievement*. Nottingham: DfES.

Department for Education and Skills (DfES) (2007) *Contextual Added Value (CAV) Information*. Nottingham: DfES.

Dyson, A. (2001) 'Special needs education as the way to equity: An alternative approach?' *Support for Learning*, 16(3): 99–104.

Dyson, L. (1997) 'An ethic of caring: Conceptual and practical issues.' *Nursing Enquiry*, 4: 196–201.

Gilligan, C. (1993) *In a Different Voice*. Cambridge, MA: Harvard University Press.

Grace, G. (1998) 'Realising the mission: Catholic approaches to school effectiveness.' In R. Slee, G. Weiner and S. Tomlinson (eds) *School Effectiveness for Whom?* London: Falmer.

Held, V. (1993) *Feminist Morality*. Chicago, IL: University of Chicago Press.

Hurd, T. and Brabeck, M. (1997) 'Presentations of women and Gilligan's ethic of care in college textbooks, 1970–1999: An examination of bias.' *Teaching of Psychology*, 24(3): 159–167.

Lloyd, L. (2004) 'Mortality and morality: Aging and the ethics of care.' *Ageing and Society*, 24: 235–256.

Moss, P. (2001) 'Making space for ethics.' *Australian Journal of Early Childhood*, 26(4): 1–6.

Nias, J. (1999) 'Primary teaching as a culture of care.' In J. Prosser (ed.) *School Culture*. London: Paul Chapman.

Noddings, N. (2005) 'Identifying and responding to needs in education.' *Cambridge Journal of Education*, 35(2): 147–159.

Ofsted (2006) *Extended Services in Schools and Children's Centres*. London: Ofsted.

Parsons, C. (1999) 'Social inclusion and school improvement.' *Support for Learning*, 14(4): 179–183.

Sevenhuijsen, S. (2003) 'The place of care.' *Feminist Theory*, 4(2): 179–197.

Tarvis, C. (1992) *The Mismeasure of Women*. New York: Simon & Schuster.

Tronto, J. (1993) *Moral Boundaries: A political argument for an ethic of care.* New York: Routledge.

Verkerk, M. (2005) 'A feminist care-ethics approach to genetics.' In R. Ashcroft, A. Lucasson, M. Verkerk and G. Widdersharen (eds) *Case Analysis in Clinical Ethics.* Cambridge: Cambridge University Press.

Vitton, C. and Wasonga, T. (2009) 'Between Kohlberg and Gilligan: Levels of moral judgement among elementary school principals.' *Leadership and Policy in Schools,* 8: 92–116.

Vogt, F. (2002) 'A caring teacher: Explorations into primary school teachers' professional identity and ethic of care.' *Gender and Education,* 14(3): 251–264.

Wall, K. (2003) *Special Needs and Early Years.* London: Paul Chapman.

Wedell, K. (2005) 'Dilemmas in the quest for Inclusion.' *British Journal of Special Education,* 32(1): 3–10.

Index

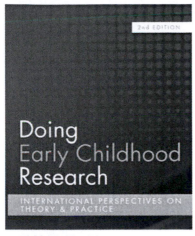

Glenda Mac Naughton
Sharne A. Rolfe
Iram Siraj-Blatchford

DOING EARLY CHILDHOOD RESEARCH

Glenda Mac Naughton

978-0-335-24262-7 (Paperback)
July 2010

"It is rare for any research methodology book to cover so much ground, and contain so many different kinds of resources between two covers."
Journal of Education for Teaching

The book provides a thorough introduction to the most common research methods used in the early childhood context. The book covers a wide range of conventional and newer methods including:

- Observation
- Surveys and interviews with adults and children
- Action research
- Ethnography
- Quasi-experimental approaches

Doing Early Childhood Research explains clearly how to set up research projects which are theoretically grounded, well-designed, rigorously analysed, feasible and ethically based. Each chapter is illustrated with examples.

www.openup.co.uk

OPEN UNIVERSITY PRESS
McGraw - Hill Education

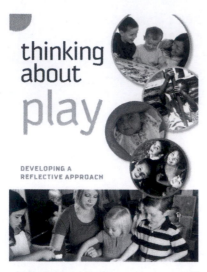

Edited by Janet Moyles

THINKING ABOUT PLAY

Janet Moyles (Editor)

978-0-335-24108-8 (Paperback)
2010

eBook also available

This edited collection brings together play and reflective practice and supports practitioners in reflecting more deeply on the play provision they make for young children. This involves analysing and evaluating what makes quality play and learning experiences by considering how current research might impact on practice.

Key features:

- Introduces the concept of 'playful pedagogies' and explains how it relates to practice
- Each chapter starts with an abstract so that readers can dip into issues of particular interest and concern
- Includes questions and follow-up ideas that can be used for CPD experiences and training

This important book supports early years students and practitioners in developing their own thinking, ideologies and pedagogies.

www.openup.co.uk